Using the Bible
for All Who Teach

Donald L. Griggs

Series editor:
Wendy S. Robins

Bible Society

This publication by the Bible Society
146 Queen Victoria Street, London EC4V 4BX

ISBN 0 564 07042 4

Contents

The Author

Donald Griggs is Director of Continuing Education and Professor of Christian Education in Richmond, Virginia, U.S.A. He and his wife, Pat, have conducted numerous workshops for Church teachers in various parts of America. They have developed a collection of resources to accompany these training events which include books, pamphlets, filmstrips, cassettes and other instructional aids.

Also by Donald Griggs in the *Using the Bible Series: In Teaching* and *With Audio-Visuals*

Editor's Note

Throughout this book, we have decided to keep the American edition's usage of the terms "goals" and "objectives", as defined in chapter 4. These may differ from British usage, which is often the reverse.

Foreword to the British Edition

"... in the third place teachers ..." Paul said (1 Corinthians 12.28). That is quite high. Only apostles and prophets are ahead of teachers in importance and there are not too many apostles and prophets around. Teaching the Bible is an indispensable activity in the progress of Christianity. This manual is a unique guide for those who want to teach the Bible in school and Sunday school but equally from the pulpit, in groups and in every kind of Bible class.

Donald Griggs gives a vision of the possibilities in Bible teaching that are within the reach of anyone who is prepared to work at it and see his task as a whole.

He shows not only how single lessons can be creatively handled but how in time a whole Bible world-view can be communicated and absorbed. To achieve this he introduces practical ways to plan for teaching. After you have read the book it will be clear in Bible teaching as in other fields "If you fail to plan, you plan to fail".

The Bible suffers a much harder lot than any of the martyrs because its martyrdom is perpetual and often at the hands of its professional teachers, ministers and priests. If a significant number of the clergy were to read and apply the wisdom in this book in their churches, the fortunes of Christianity in Britain would improve drastically.

Tom Houston
Executive Director
Bible Society

Introduction

Teaching is not so much a science as it is an art. The teacher is more an artist than he is a scientist. There are too many variables, too many unpredictable factors in just one hour of classroom activities for us to become scientific about teaching and learning. If teaching were a science, then all we would have to do is master the proper formulae for a given situation and we would be guaranteed success. But teaching is not a science; there is no one right way to teach a given class or a particular subject, or to approach a group of students. Teaching is an art that must be developed, practised, and evaluated.

Even though teaching is not a science, there are many techniques which teachers can employ that will lead to more effective teaching. Art has its structure and style. There is a discipline which every artist accepts. There are rules to follow and criteria to consider. That is true of teaching also.

This manual is an attempt to identify and systematize some of the basic elements of Christian teaching and learning. We cannot cover everything but we can uncover some of the essential ingredients for effective teaching. The manual is designed for people who are regularly involved in teaching the Bible, and is especially suitable for those responsible for planning teaching and learning activities that last for more than an hour a week.

The focus in the first two chapters is on the role of the teacher and the decisions that the teacher must make from week to week. The next six chapters focus on the planning process and the essential components of every lesson plan. If two or more teachers read through these six chapters together then they can plan the activities together as a team. There are suggested exercises for each person to do to practise the planning process. In chapters nine to twelve, four general topics are presented which offer suggestions to teachers of ways to implement specific techniques and resources in their teaching. Chapter thirteen has six sections which are designed particularly for those who are concerned about providing support and training for the teachers for whom they are responsible. The last section offers ten designs for teacher education events based upon the content of the first twelve chapters.

In this manual I have, for myself and others, gathered together a lot of my ideas and teaching strategies. It will be most useful if the reader works through one chapter at a time, beginning with the first. The church leader could start with chapter thirteen, but that chapter will make more sense after reading the first twelve chapters.

The term ''students'' is used throughout to refer to anyone involved in the learning situation, regardless of their age. I have used the term ''curriculum'' to refer to commercially produced source materials and to the lesson plans prepared by teachers for use in their own classes.

1

Roles of the Teacher

Teachers perform many roles in the classroom. After a busy session with paint, poster, or collage materials the teacher may feel that the role of a cleaner is most fitting. Or when a student is troubled and needs someone to talk to, the role of counsellor may be most appropriate. We could probably list a dozen or more roles teachers take in the course of several sessions of teaching. In this chapter we want to focus on four especially important roles.

Friend

Perhaps the most important role a teacher can play is that of being a **friend** to the students. We are not talking about a false, over-friendly relationship, but we are emphasizing the personal, caring, loving, "being-with" sort of relationship that helps people learn how to communicate with each other and grow together. Think for a moment about the teachers you had while a student at church or school. Try to think especially about one or two particular teachers whom you would have called friends. What do you recall about them as people, or about the way they behaved, that makes you think of them as friends? I have asked many people this question and their replies have included comments such as:
"We had opportunities to know them outside the class."
"Mrs._____always called us by name."
"Sometimes Mr._____ would visit us and our parents at home."
"They really listened and cared about what we had to say."
"They were interested in the things that we were interested in."
    I am sure you could add your own observations to the list of things that make you remember certain teachers as friends. Most students will be taught by many different teachers. What a tragedy it would be if some of those teachers were not remembered as friends.
    The important point is that we have a chance to be remembered by the students we teach as people who are their friends. The students will remember us as people long after they have forgotten the specific subjects we have taught.
    Even though this whole manual is focused upon skills, techniques, activities and resources that contribute to effective teaching we must always remember that the relationships we establish in our classrooms are of primary importance. God has always worked and spoken through people. In the classrooms we teach in, we are the people through whom God will speak to boys and girls, men and women.

Translator

Another important role of the teacher is that of **translator.** Teachers are much better as translators than they are as transmitters. A transmitter sends messages in one direction, from the source to the receiver. The problem with this mode of communication is that the success of the communication rests in the hands of the receiver. The receiver can decide whether or not to tune in, whether to switch channels or whether to turn the volume up or down. From what I have seen in many classrooms, I am sure that behaviour which is often identified as a discipline problem is not really that, but rather an example of what happens when a student changes channels or tunes out from a transmitter teacher.

The teacher will be much more effective as a translator. A translator is someone who helps facilitate communication between people who are otherwise unable to communicate with each other. The translator has to listen very carefully. The translator must be familiar with the languages, frames of reference, and background of both parties. This is what is needed in the church: teachers who listen, teachers who are familiar with both the world of the church

and the world of the student. If teachers work as translators, they will find that students become much more involved and motivated to learn.

Curriculum writer

The third role of the teacher is that of **curriculum writer.** Even if the teacher is using pre-prepared materials, these are often very general and need to be adapted for use with the teacher's own class. Only the individual teacher can determine whether or not a particular activity is appropriate for all, some or none of his class, and it is in this sense that the teacher is a curriculum writer.

If we said that one of the roles of the teacher is lesson planner that would be no surprise or shock. Well, the lesson that is planned and used with a group of students is the curriculum they experience. Therefore, teachers must be helped to think and make decisions in the way that curriculum writers do.

The next chapter focuses on ten curriculum decisions that teachers must make. This whole manual is intended to help teachers to become more skilful as curriculum writers.

Learner

The fourth role of the teacher is that of a **learner.** Teachers will be continually learning about children, about teaching, and about biblical and theological concepts, and so furthering their own education.

When teachers serve as friends, translators, curriculum writers and learners then we can almost guarantee that teaching and learning will be exciting and rewarding for both teachers and students.

2

Ten Curriculum Decisions

In the process of producing a teaching plan and implementing it, teachers must make many decisions. Even without a plan in an informal setting teachers must decide:

○ Who will I ask next?

○ What questions will I ask?

○ How can I get Andy more involved?

○ What will I say in response to that question?

Consciously or unconsciously, teachers are called upon to make many decisions in the course of an hour's session. A problem many of us face as teachers is that we do not deliberately consider several alternative actions or responses, then choose the one that is most appropriate. Many times we react too quickly and do the first thing that comes to mind. With a little more careful

planning and an awareness of some of the more important decisions that must be made, all teachers can become more effective in their teaching.

The ten decisions in the following outline are not the only ones that a teacher will have to make. However, these are some of the most important decisions. Keeping the checklist of questions in mind when planning and teaching may help the teacher to teach more purposefully. Each of the ten decisions, or areas of concern, is explored more thoroughly in other chapters in this manual. Also, there are a number of books which can help a teacher explore more thoroughly each of the subjects. (See Bibliography.)

1. What will I teach?

○ The curriculum is a starting place, but it contains too much material.
○ I must select the key concepts on which to focus my teaching.
○ Concepts are words that people use to represent experience, thoughts, objects, etc., to communicate with others.
○ Concepts are the focus of all teaching.
○ It is important to relate concepts to the life-experience of the students.

2. What will the students learn?

○ It is important for teachers to have clear objectives in mind towards which they can direct their planning and teaching.
○ Objectives express what teachers intend the students to achieve in a period of instruction.
○ Objectives should be specific in terms of what the students will do.
○ Objectives help the teacher to evaluate what happened.

3. What teaching activities will I plan for the session?

○ A variety of teaching activities will involve most of the students most of the time.
○ Teaching activities should represent different levels of interest and ability.
○ New activities should be introduced and tried out regularly.

4. What resources will the students and I use?

○ Resources are not just gimmicks and gadgets.
○ Resources are those means by which students get involved in their own learning.
○ Resources must be selected carefully.
○ Resources are for students and teachers.
○ A wide variety of resources should be used.

5. What strategy will I use to get students involved?

○ It takes a carefully worked out strategy to engage the students with interest and purpose in their study.
○ There are at least five elements to the strategy which include Opening,

Presentation, Exploration, Creativity and Closing.

6. How will the room be arranged?
○ The room arrangement, decoration, and display of resources teach as much as the words we use.
○ Allow for maximum visibility of all materials and easy movement of all students.
○ Rearrange the furniture, equipment, displays, and materials regularly.

7. What questions will I ask?
○ Questions are an important, necessary activity.
○ It will help to plan key questions ahead of time.
○ There are at least three levels of questions to use which include Information, Analytical and Personal questions.

8. What choices will the students make during the session?
○ Student choices lead to greater motivation and involvement.
○ Choices should be considered for every step of the lesson plan.
○ Choices need to be discussed and evaluated.

9. What instructions will I give?
○ The success of students in the learning activities is often determined by the kind of instructions that the teacher gives.
○ The teacher's instructions guide the students.
○ Directions should be visible as well as verbal.
○ Directions should be given in several steps.

10. How will I respond after a student says or does something?
○ The teacher should encourage the student as this will lead to greater participation.
○ Students need to receive feedback or responses from their teachers.
○ Teachers can develop a repertoire of responses.

The rest of this manual is intended to help teachers explore further the subject of each of these decisions or questions.

3 Focus on Key Concepts

To focus on key concepts is to respond to the question raised in the first of the teacher's decisions listed in chapter two: *What will I teach?*

Before planning a lesson or entering the classroom the teacher must consider the subject matter to be taught. There are various sources to help the teacher decide what to teach. The source material itself, the season of the year, current events in the world, nation, or community, the suggestions of ministers and church leaders, as well as the needs and interests of the students, all influence to some degree what will be taught.

Most teachers have commented, "There is too much to teach. I will never be able to cover it all if I had twice as much time." That is true! There is too much to teach. Teachers must participate actively and responsibly in the process of deciding what to teach. Teachers need to be selective. Since they cannot teach everything, then teachers should select key concepts which will provide a focus for one or more sessions.

If teachers are tempted to try and cover everything, remember that one meaning of "cover" is to hide something from view and this is exactly what can happen. The task of the teacher instead is to "uncover . . .", "to uncover" key concepts so that they can be presented, understood, and used with clarity and meaning.

When selecting which key concepts to teach, teachers must be concerned about several factors.

Concepts are basic to our teaching in the church. The dictionary defines "concept" as a "thought or an opinion: a mental image of a thing formed by generalization from particulars." Something that is omitted from this definition is that concepts are mostly derived from one's experience. A person's experiences of "love," "church," "father" will influence to a large degree his concepts of them. In teaching in the church we confront students who bring with them a wide variety of experiences with already-formed concepts so that the process of communication and teaching is not an easy one.

Consider, for example, the concept of "shepherd" in "the Lord is my shepherd." For a nomadic Hebrew who lived with sheep, who was either himself a shepherd or whose family included some shepherds, it was not difficult to think of God as being like a shepherd.

God guides, cares for, and protects people the way a shepherd provides for his sheep. But what about a child in an urban or suburban community who has never seen, touched, heard, or smelled a sheep, or who has never seen a shepherd? How can he form an appropriate concept of shepherd as intended in Psalm 23? The only concept of shepherd one girl had was that her pet dog was a German shepherd. She was really confused when she was first introduced to "the Lord is my shepherd."

What this suggests to me is that concepts taught in the church will be more easily grasped if they can somehow be related to the experience level of the students. Shepherd to a Hebrew in Israel was a very concrete, real concept, but to an urban student it is a very abstract concept. The more abstract a concept is, the more open it is to misunderstanding and the more difficult it is to teach.

A. **Start where the learner is.** As teachers we have become very familiar with concepts like "God is love," "The Bible is the word of God," and many more. However, for students there is not the same familiarity. Students in our classes will hear for the first time concepts that are very familiar to us. But we must start where the learner is, building concepts on experiences that are appropriate to the learner.

B. **Begin with concepts based upon the learner's experience.** If students come to the classroom knowing only a little about the Moses stories, then we can be the means of telling them more. Before talking about the Hebrews as slaves we need to be sure the students can define what a slave is.

C. **Reinforce what is taught by comparison and repetition.** The parables of Jesus are good examples of this process. Students learn quickly and what they learn is retained when they are actively involved in the process of comparing factors related to the particular concepts. Repetition need not be boring recitation, but rather a re-working of the same material in a different way.

D. **Be selective; focus on one concept at a time.** We tend to try to teach too much. When we introduce a hundred concepts in an hour, we are sure to confuse the student. We need to be selective by teaching a few key concepts well and not worrying about all those other concepts that were not included in this session. Better to teach a few concepts well than to cover dozens of concepts lightly.

An activity to practise focusing on key concepts
Take time to do the following activity which helps to reinforce some of the things we have considered in focusing on key concepts.

Step One
Make a list of key words

In the blank space below or on a piece of paper write down five or six key words that you would use to say something important about **Jesus.**

Jesus

1.   4.

2.   5.

3.   6.

Step Two
Compare your lists of words

If you are doing this with another person, or several others, compare your lists of five or six words with each other. If you are doing this activity by yourself then compare your list of five or six words with my words. As you compare your lists, look to see how many of your words are similar to or different from the other's.

My list of words focusing on **Jesus:**

1. teacher   4. alive today
2. God's representative   5. suffering servant
3. Messiah   6. truly man

Step Three
Consider two factors

As a result of what we have just done there are two factors worth considering:

1. No two people choose exactly the same five or six key concepts to focus on Jesus. The more people participating in the activity the bigger the total number of words will be.

If we really do have different concepts that are important to each of us, then how can we ever assume that our particular way of thinking or expressing ourselves about Jesus is the only way or the right way?

This is a good demonstration of why the teacher must act as a *translator* (listening to and accepting the student's way of thinking) rather than as a transmitter (assuming that what a teacher has to say is the only way or the best way).

2. Even though no two lists are identical, there will probably be one or two words that are similar when we compare two or more lists.

This suggests that even though we think and express ourselves in unique ways there is much that we have in common on a given subject. We do have concepts that we share and this is a good place to begin in our study and work together.

This is another good example of why it is important to be a translator — to start where the other person is, to begin with what we have in common, and to build upon that.

Step Four
Make a composite list

On a blackboard, a piece of paper or in this manual, make a composite list of all the words from the several lists. If it is just you and me, then combine our two lists to use for the next step.

List all the words:
- teacher
-
-
- God's representative
-
- Messiah

- alive today
-
- suffering servant
-
-
- truly man

Step Five
Put all the concepts
in two categories

Look at all the words and place each in one of two categories: *concrete* or *abstract*. Concrete concepts are related to direct experiences; you can close your eyes and have a mental image of a concrete concept. You can draw a picture of a concrete concept. Abstract concepts are more symbolic; it takes more abstract concepts to explain or describe an abstract concept.

When you put the list of words in these two categories what do you notice? Are most of the words in the *abstract* category? If so, this is not surprising because we are adults, and as adults we have become able to think abstractly and to use abstract concepts with meaning.

But that is not true of younger students or those unfamiliar with these concepts. People begin to make sense of concepts when they can connect the concepts to something concrete, to something in their own experience.

Step Six
Relate concepts that
belong together

Look at the list of words again. Select three or more words from the list that have something in common with each other. Then give that list of words a title. The title for the words will indicate how they belong together in one category. For example, if we had in one list the words: "teaches, preaches, leads, and prays" we could give them the title **Actions of Jesus** or **Works of Jesus.**

Work on your own category of words and title.

Title: _____

1.   4.
2.   5.
3.   6.

You can add some other words to your category that were not in the original list.

This is an example of one way that you can decide what to teach; select concepts and focus on those that belong together. It is more helpful to students to work with concepts that have a connection with each other than to work with random sets of concepts.

Step Seven
Summarize the category
with a statement

Now that you have a set of words that belong together in one category, imagine that you have a group of students to whom you want to communicate these concepts. Write two or three sentences, keeping them as simple, concrete, and as connected to the central category as possible. The statement should be an expression of what you believe is important, that summarizes the essence of what you want to communicate.

Write your own statement . . .

These seven steps represent a process that helps a teacher respond to the question, ''What will I teach?'' Also, these steps suggest that it is important for teachers to respond to the question as *translators* and not as transmitters.

There will be another opportunity to put into practice what we have learned about key concepts when we get to chapter seven, *Practise the Planning Process.*

4

Focus on Instructional Objectives

Whenever we plan a trip, a special meal, or a project around the house we usually have some specific objectives* in mind: to arrive at the coast on June 15th, to have ten guests for dinner to be served at 7 p.m., or to finish painting the outside of the house during the two weeks' holiday. It is very easy to evaluate whether or not we achieved these objectives. Obviously, the objectives are not achieved just because we have set them. It takes a lot of planning in order to achieve our intended objectives.

Objectives in teaching are somewhat similar. What we want to achieve with the students should be as specific as possible. We should be able to determine at the end of a session or unit of instruction whether or not the objectives for the students have been achieved.

A. First, some words of **definition:**

1. **Objective** (noun)

"An object to be won; purpose of a plan." (Longman Dictionary of Contemporary English)

2. **Objective** (noun)

"A collection of words describing a teacher's intent for the student."

(Robert F. Mager — see Bibliography)

3. "**Behavioural objectives** are statements which describe what students will be able to do after completing a prescribed unit of instruction."

(Kibler, Barker, and Miles — educational specialists)

B. **Compare goals with objectives**

As teachers we usually have some goals in mind that we could specify if someone asked us. Often we use the words "goals" and "objectives" synonymously. I think it is very important to distinguish the differences between goals and objectives. See the diagram *Comparing goals and objectives,* which attempts to summarize these differences.

C. Next, the **criteria for writing** instructional objectives:

1. An objective should be written in terms of **student** performance. Does it say what we expect of the student?

2. An objective should state in **observable** terms what students will be expected to do. Does it describe something we can *see* or *hear* the students do?

3. An objective should be **specific.** Does it describe clearly and specifically what is expected of the student?

4. An objective should state something of the **conditions** within the

*Please see Editor's Note on page 3.

student will be expected to perform. Does it indicate the condition that will influence a student's action?

Comparing Goals and Objectives

Goals . . . are big enough to spend a whole lifetime pursuing.

. . . are beyond our reach; we will never fully achieve the goals of Christian living.

. . . give us direction for our teaching, learning, relating, deciding, etc.

. . . are too general to use for planning and evaluating teaching activities.

Many of the factors that help people to achieve a goal are outside the sphere of influence of the teacher.

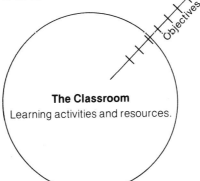

A Goal

"People will become more loving and caring towards other people."
(sample goal)

The Classroom
Learning activities and resources.

Objectives . . . are specific

. . . are written in terms of what students can be expected to accomplish, in particular learning activities.

. . . are achievable.

. . . are just little steps along the way towards the larger goal.

. . . are very helpful guidelines for teachers to use in planning and evaluating teaching activities.

The teacher's work directly helps people to achieve their objectives.

"At the end of the period of study, the students will visit an elderly person from the church to give them a gift and make conversation with that person."
(sample objective)

---

5. An objective should be **measurable**. Does it include a statement of quality of level of intended performance?

6. An objective should be **sequential** in relation to previous and following objectives. Does it relate in sequence to what preceded and what is to follow?

D. **Start writing an objective** with the following statement:

"At the end of the session(s) the students should be able to . . ."

Comment: This is a very helpful way to begin every instructional objective. It focuses on the *student* and what the teacher intends him to be able to *do*.

E. After this introductory statement, **the next word is the key to the whole objective.**

Avoid using words that are general and non-specific, as in the following:

At the end of the session(s) the students should be able to:
understand . . .
know . . .
believe . . .
realize . . .
appreciate . . .
feel . . .
acknowledge . . .

Comment: These words are too general. They are goal-oriented words. They do not help teachers determine whether students have accomplished what was intended. There is nothing wrong with "understanding," etc., per se, but as guidelines in planning for and evaluating teaching they are not very helpful.

Instead, **be specific** as follows:

At the end of the session(s) the students should be able to:

demonstrate . . .	list . . .	cite . . .
compare . . .	describe . . .	follow . . .
identify . . .	show . . .	quote . . .
state . . .	organize . . .	name . . .
create . . .	write . . .	summarize . . .
explain . . .	express . . .	contribute . . .
present . . .	suggest . . .	participate . . .
apply . . .	locate . . .	select . . .
find . . .	discuss . . .	ask . . .

Comment: All the above words are actions students can do which can be *seen* or *heard* by teachers. Such actions by students provide clues to the teacher that enable the teacher to evaluate more objectively whether or not students have achieved what was intended.

An activity to practise writing instructional objectives

Step One
Compare two statements

Read the following two statements and compare the differences between them.

(1) The purpose of the class period is to help the students learn how to use a Bible Concordance.

(2) At the end of the session the students should be able to use a Bible Concord-

ance to find five familiar passages of scripture related to the word "covenant."

Some questions to consider:
○ What differences have you noticed?
○ Which statement is the more general?
○ Which statement is more directed to student activity?
○ Which statement would be more helpful after the session to guide the teacher in evaluating whether or not the objective was achieved?

The second statement is the better of the two because it is more specific, more focused on student activity and more helpful for later evaluation.

Step Two
Compare two more statements

Read the following two statements and compare them.

(1) At the end of the session the students should be able to **list** six different actions and/or teachings of both Amos and Jeremiah and to **compare** the differences and similarities between them.

(2) At the end of the session the students should be able to **understand** some of the important teachings of the prophets Amos and Jeremiah.

Some questions to consider:
○ What do you notice about these two statements when you compare them?
○ Which objective states actions of the students that can be seen or heard?
○ Which objectives would be more helpful in evaluating the students' achievements?

The first statement is the better of the two because it states in observable terms what a student is expected to do.

A summary statement

The two sets of examples of objectives given above focus on the two primary, essential criteria for writing objectives. Objectives should be **written for students in terms of their action,** and **written with student actions that can be observed** (that is, we can actually see and/or hear what the students do). These two elements should always be included whenever writing objectives.

There are two other criteria which help make objectives more specific and achievable: **the conditions under which they will be achieved** and **the quality of achievement expected by the teacher.** These two criteria will clarify the objectives, but need not be included in every objective a teacher writes.

Step Three
Two additional criteria
for writing objectives

A. The conditions by which objectives will be achieved include time, materials and resources. In the following objectives the conditions are printed in bold.

(1) By using a **Bible dictionary** and **commentary (given 30 minutes)** the students should be able to write a two-paragraph interpretation of Psalm 23 in their own words.

(2) Given a **blank map** of the lands of the Bible the students should be able to locate accurately all the following places: Dead Sea, River Jordan, Egypt, Sea of Galilee and and the Sinai Peninsula.

B. The quality with which objectives will be achieved says something of the level of expectation that a teacher has. In the following objectives the words which indicate **quality** are printed in bold.

(1) By using a Bible dictionary and commentary (given 30 minutes) the students should be able to write a **two paragraph** interpretation of Psalm 23 in **their own words.**

(2) Given a blank map of the lands of the Bible the students should be able to locate **accurately all** the following places . . .

Step Four
Practise writing
your own objectives

Use the following main idea as a basis for writing a set of objectives.

"Jesus called people to become his disciples. Twelve men were specifically chosen to learn from and work with Jesus. Jesus needs disciples today to learn from him and work for love, peace, and justice."

Write several objectives based upon the above main idea:

At the end of the session the students should be able to:
1.
2.
3.
4.

5 Focus on Teaching-learning Activities

Once the **key concepts** are focused and the **instructional objectives** determined, the teacher should have a clear sense of direction. The next step in planning is to design the **teaching activities** that will most effectively communicate the concepts and achieve the objectives. The accent is upon **activity.**

If a teacher begins to prepare for a lesson by asking, "What am I going to say to the class about the concept of covenant?" then they are beginning by asking the wrong sort of question. It is wrong because it leads the teacher to believe that the teacher is going to *tell the students*. It is more appropriate to ask, "What are *we* going to do in order to learn about the concept of covenant?"

Answering this question leads directly to thinking about activities, what people will be doing in the classroom to learn.

Teaching activities are defined as all those actions of students and teachers that aid learning. There are dozens of possible teaching activities that can be organized into several categories as illustrated by the diagram below.

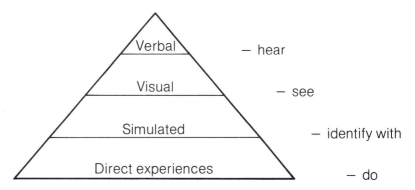

Verbal	— hear
Visual	— see
Simulated	— identify with
Direct experiences	— do

Verbal activities have been the most common means used in teaching. Teaching activities in this category are: lecture, discussion, records, tapes, sermon, story, reading, and any other type of verbal presentation that depends primarily upon the hearing of the learner. The evidence is that most people do not learn well just through listening to something. In order to be effective, verbal activities must be accompanied by other types of activity. Hearing for most people is a passive activity not requiring much participation from the learner. Also, hearing is very selective. We tend to hear what we want to hear.

Another category of teaching activities is the use of visual symbols. **Visual symbols** involve the learner in looking at things. Activities in this category are: use of teaching pictures, filmstrips, map study, films, looking at books, and many other types of visual presentations. Most people learn more from what they see than from what they hear. Seeing is less passive than hearing. Seeing elicits a response from the one who sees. When verbal and visual symbols are used together in a combined activity, the learning is more effective than when either is used separately.

Simulated experiences move us a step further on from verbal and visual activities. To simulate is to act out what is unreal as if it were real. Teaching activities in this category are role play, drama, simulation games, some field trips, some creative writing and other experiences which place students in the position of acting out particular feelings, problems, or issues. An example of a simulated experience using creative writing would be where a student assumes the role of Moses at the time he has returned to Egypt to seek freedom for the

Hebrew slaves. Moses has confronted Pharaoh, who has refused to let the people go and instead has increased their work load. Pharaoh is uncooperative. The Hebrew people are angry at Moses and Moses wonders whether or not God is going to keep his promise. That is the situation to be simulated. The students are directed to write a letter, as Moses would write, to his wife, father-in-law or friend back in Midian. In doing this assignment one student addressed his letter, "Dear Sheep . . ." A simulated activity involves the students more significantly in developing and identifying with the concepts of the session.

Direct experiences are those activities when students are actually involved in real situations, problems, and concepts. Because so many concepts in religious teaching tend to be abstract it is often difficult to design direct experience teaching activities.

An example in working on the concept of "love your neighbour as yourself" would be for the students to visit a Convalescent Home or other shut-ins in order to show them that caring can be practical.

We can talk about "love your neighbour" in a long discussion and the chances are that it will make little impression. We could select pictures from magazines to illustrate examples of people caring for others and the meaning would be more memorable. We could act out or write endings to several open-ended stories illustrating people needing love and this gets closer to the meaning of the concept. Or, we could go as a class, or in small groups, to visit some people who really need love from a neighbour. Which activity would require the most involvement on the part of the students? Which activity would be the most memorable? Probably the visit to the shut-ins. Also, the next time the students hear "and you shall love your neighbour as yourself" they will probably remember that visit and relate it to the concepts of "love" and "neighbour"

The more our teaching activities use verbal symbols the less involved the students are and the less they will learn. The more our teaching moves towards direct and simulated experiences the more involved the student will be in his own learning. Too much talking by the teacher makes it harder for the students to get really involved, whereas teaching activities which involve direct experiences tend to include all the students in one way or another.

We suggested earlier that a teacher begin his planning by asking, "What are we going to do?" There is another helpful question a teacher can ask: "What direct experience will best communicate the concept I want to teach?" Direct experiences cannot always be thought of, nor are they always feasible or appropriate. Then we should consider what simulated experiences are possible. Verbal activities should be employed only after other activities have been used. Verbal activities should never be used exclusively for a whole instructional period for any age group. It is best when there is a variety of activities in a session involving all the students in several different ways.

Deciding which teaching activity to use is a necessary task that all teachers must perform.

Here are some criteria that can be used in deciding which teaching activities to employ:

1. The activity should involve most of the students in an active way.
2. It should be an activity in which the teacher has some confidence.
3. It should allow for maximum creativity on the part of the students.
4. It should not be so familiar as to bore the students.
5. If it is a new activity, students should have the opportunity to experiment with it in order to discover its possibilities.
6. There should usually be a variety of activities offered so that students can have a choice.
7. The activity should contribute directly to communicating the key concepts and achieving the specific objectives.
8. The activity should lead the students to seek answers, state conclusions or express creative responses.
9. Whatever activities are designed should be appropriate to the ages and skills of the students involved.

By using these criteria, teachers should be able to design teaching activities that will involve the students in the process of their own learning.

Ideas or suggestions for possible teaching activities come from many sources:

○ Commercially prepared materials
○ other teachers
○ past experiences
○ educational magazines, journals, books
○ state school teachers
○ training events

Teachers need always to be alert to new ways of designing teaching activities. By reading, sharing and experiencing a variety of activities teachers will become more resourceful in their planning and teaching.

Samples of ways to organize teaching-learning activities

Every lesson plan has a beginning, middle, and end. There are many different activities that are appropriate for beginning, developing and ending a lesson. The five stages in a typical lesson plan are outlined in what follows.

1. **Opening the session** The first thing that teachers and students do in a

session is one of the most important activities of the whole hour. The opening section can be as brief as one minute or as long as ten minutes.

2. **Presenting the subject** Before students can begin to work meaningfully, it is helpful to present them with some basic information about the concepts to be developed in the session.

3. **Exploring the subject** Students are more stimulated to learn when they are able to work individually or in small groups to explore further the subject matter that is the focus of the day's session.

4. **Responding creatively** Learning is reinforced and students are able to express themselves in meaningful ways when they are encouraged to respond in one or more creative ways to what they have learned.

5. **Concluding the session** Each session should be brought to a fitting conclusion so that students sense a completeness to the sequence of learning activities experienced that day.

Even though there is something of a logical sequence to these five parts of a lesson plan it is possible that the Presenting, Exploring and Responding activities could be experienced in a variety of combinations. It is possible that Presenting and Exploring activities could happen simultaneously, e.g. when students are researching a subject using a variety of resources. Also, Exploring and Responding activities may happen together, e.g. when students are writing their own script for selected frames of a filmstrip.

There are many different teaching-learning activities that can be used in each of these five parts of a lesson plan.

Some ways to open the session

○ Students read a definition of a concept and ask questions.
○ The teacher reads a story or passage of scripture and asks questions.
○ Students listen to a recording: song, story, commentary or other pre-recorded material.
○ Students view a film or filmstrips which introduces the subject.
○ Teacher and students look at and discuss a photo or painting.
○ Students select a passage of scripture or a concept to explore further.
○ The teacher refers to recent school, church, or community events.
○ Teacher and students brainstorm a subject.
○ The teacher involves students in a voting activity.
○ The teacher uses a newspaper or magazine article or photo.
○ (add your own)

Some ways to present the subject

○ The teacher makes a brief presentation (lecture).

○ Students read a selection from scripture or another resource book.

○ Students watch a film or filmstrip.

○ Students listen to a tape recording of a story, sermon, scripture, commentary, report, etc.

○ Students present brief reports that are previously prepared.

○ Guest speaker or other resource people present the subject through lecture, interview, panel, debate, etc.

○ The teacher reads or tells a story.

○ Teacher or students present a puppet play.

○ The teacher involves students in an exercise to help them to clarify their values (see *Using the Bible In Teaching,* chapter nine).

○ Students go on a field trip.

○ (add your own).

Some ways to explore the subject

○ Students do research in the Bible and/or other resource books.

○ Students write scripts for filmstrips, slides, puppet plays or other dramas.

○ Students use photos or other materials to select visual expressions of a concept.

○ Students interview other people and record interview (see *Using the Bible with Audio-Visuals,* chapter two).

○ Students discuss with the teacher and other students.

○ Students use prepared worksheets (see *Using the Bible in Teaching*).

○ Students select a learning centre in which to work.

○ Students participate in a simulation game.

○ Students listen to pre-recorded resources.
○ Students do an exercise to help them to clarify their values (see *Using the Bible in Teaching,* chapter nine).
○ (add your own).

Some ways to respond creatively
○ Writing activities (e.g. letters, reports, poems, newspapers, scripts).
○ Write-on slides, filmstrip and film activities (see *Using the Bible with Audio-Visuals).*
○ Recording activities (e.g. news reports, scripts, songs, drama, interview).
○ Construction activities (e.g. scale models, maps, three-dimensional objects).

○ Drama activities (e.g. role play, puppets, dance, pantomime, drama).
○ Painting or drawing activities.
○ Photographic activities (e.g. slides, photos, 8mm films, polaroid camera).
○ Collage (e.g. felt, natural materials, junk, photos).
○ Multi-media activities.
○ (add your own).

Some ways to conclude the session

○ Each student shares his creativity.
○ Teacher leads discussion in which students express their own ideas.
○ Teacher and/or students prepare for time of worship.
○ Teacher summarizes.
○ Students complete unfinished sentences.

○ Teacher and/or students close with prayer.
○ Teacher and students sing song together.
○ Whole class meditates in silence for one minute.
○ Students lead a time of celebration.
○ Students decide on a project or action for next week.
○ (add your own).

Practise focusing on teaching-learning activities
Here is a series of activities that you could use to help you focus on teaching-learning activities.

Activity one

○ Look at your source material.

○ Read all the material for one unit.
○ Write down on a blank sheet of paper all the activities that are suggested for the unit.
○ Categorize all the activities according to Verbal, Visual, Simulated or Direct experiences:

Activity two

○ As Activity one.
○ Then, categorize all the activities according to the five parts of a lesson plan: Opening, Presenting, Exploring, Responding and Closing.

Activity three

○ Read again the suggestions under each of the above five parts of a lesson.
○ In the blank to the left of each suggestion place a tick ($\checkmark$) for each time you have used the activity in the last six weeks.
○ If an item has three or more ticks you may be using that activity too often.

Activity four

○ Use the suggestions for the five parts of a lesson again.
○ In the blank, place a cross (x) for each activity you have never used.
○ If you have three or more crosses for one of the parts it may be that you are overlooking a very valuable activity.
○ Some of the activities are developed in greater detail in this manual. If any of the following subjects have crosses by them, you may want to read more in this manual or in other books listed in the *Bibliography* to help you gain information and confidence to try a new activity.
○ Uses of media: including slides, filmstrips, cassette recordings, films and overhead projection.
○ Values clarification strategies.
○ Asking questions and leading discussion.
○ Creative activities.

Activity five

Read the suggestions for the five parts of a lesson once more. Put a star (*) next to each of the suggestions you intend to include in your next unit of teaching.

6 Focus on Teaching-learning Resources

Teaching-learning **activities** are what teachers and students **do** in and out of the classroom to help them to communicate and learn about particular concepts. **Resources** are what teachers and students **use** in the process of teaching and learning.

Resources can be organized in the same categories as described in the preceding section on teaching-learning activities. Some examples of resources in each category are:

Resources for *verbal* activities

- ○ cassette tapes to listen to
- ○ cassette recorder for recording students' statements
- ○ record player for listening to records
- ○ pens or pencils and paper for writing activities
- ○ resource books without diagrams, maps or photos

Resources for *visual* activies

- ○ maps, charts, posters, photographs and banners
- ○ filmstrips and projectors
- ○ overhead projector and transparencies
- ○ 16mm films and projectors
- ○ 8mm cameras, films and projectors
- ○ blackboard, notice-board
- ○ books with photographs, paintings, diagrams, maps
- ○ magazine pictures
- ○ 35mm cameras, slides, projectors
- ○ write-on slides, filmstrips, and films
- ○ flannelgraph, magnetic board

Resources for *simulated* activities

- ○ puppets and stage for puppet plays
- ○ direction and supplies for simulation games
- ○ scripts, props, costumes, etc. for drama
- ○ materials for constructing scale models
- ○ resources to help students identify with a particular person, event, or concept

Resources for *direct experience* activities

- ○ All the above resources can be used to help students to do something directly related to a key concept that is connected with his own experiences.
- ○ In addition there are many resources that can help students experience learning directly.

Teachers can gather resources from many places: cupboards at home or at church, shops, denominational offices and publishers, and even the rubbish bin.

Resources can be as costly as a video-tape system and as inexpensive as a magazine.

If students are to be motivated to learn and if they are to use more than verbal symbols to express themselves, then teachers need to use a wide variety of resources.

Resources are as necessary to teaching and learning as dishes and utensils are to eating. You can survive without resources — but not without experiencing considerable frustration.

The same criteria used for determining which teaching activities to employ in the classroom may be used to decide which resources to use.

There are many books, magazines, and articles that suggest creative ways of using a wide variety of resources; for instance most teachers will have used pictures in one way or another.

Many teachers have experienced great excitement and satisfaction as they have participated with other teachers in a brainstorm session on possible ways of using a particular resource.

Teacher Survival*

Most teachers can recall vividly the first time they faced a class of students as the teacher. For some of us that was a frightening experience. I can remember my first teaching assignment. The Assistant Pastor recruited me to teach a Junior High class. He handed me a teacher's guide and some student's material, directed me to the room, showed me where to find the light switch, and said, "Good Luck!"

Quite soon I discovered that the teacher's guide and student's material were not sufficient for the task of planning to teach. I needed what all teachers need, a wide variety of resources and skills from which to select the most appropriate for a particular session. In addition to having resources available, I needed to develop some criteria for determining which resources were of highest priority and most valuable.

What follows is a simple Simulation Game to help teachers approach the business of considering the value of particular resources and setting priorities for their use. The "game" is played most profitably by four or more people.

*Teacher Survival by Donald L. Griggs, Copyright, 1970, The Arizona Experiment. Used by permission. Teacher Survival is a Simulation Game that can be used by one or more people to focus on the relative value they place on a variety of teaching-learning resources.

Worksheet needed

In preparation for playing the game, prepare copies of the worksheet below, for all players. Note the ''contingencies.''

The situation

You have moved to a remote area. (Any place where you feel isolated or alone may be remote.) A neighbour has discovered that you were involved in Christian education in the community from which you came. This new community in which you live does not have any Christian education classes and you are asked to begin one. You agree to teach, but you realize that you need some resources in order to do an effective job.

Since a friend is coming for a visit, you ask him to bring the eleven items listed on the worksheet below. On the way his car breaks down. He is going to continue the trip by bus, but he cannot bring all the resources you requested. Your friend calls long distance, and in three minutes you have to decide which items are most necessary and which items you can manage without. He can bring some items, but he is not sure how many. He will bring as many as he can, based on the order of priority you establish. (See page 38 for the next step.)

Teacher Survival Worksheet

The resources

In three minutes, rank the following items in the order of their priority of importance to you. Rank the most important item as ''1'' and the least important ''11'' and everything in between from ''2'' to ''10''.

○ Five copies of the *Good News Bible*
(a translation of the Bible in today's English).

○ Creative activities kit —
a box of materials of your choice.

○ Complete set of teacher's guides and student's material from any curriculum you may choose.

○ Record player and five records —
may include music, songs, narrations, or stories.

○ One set of pictures, posters, photos, and maps —
any combination of 20 items.

○ A hymnbook, including hymns suitable for all ages.

○ Tape recorder plus five blank one-hour tapes —
could be a small portable cassette recorder.

○ A box of old magazines —
any combination of colour supplements, woman's weeklies etc.

○ Five each of suitable editions of Bible Dictionary, Atlas, Encyclopaedia.

○ An overhead projector, with materials needed for using it.
○ Filmstrip/slide projector with five filmstrips, scripts, records and 100 miscellaneous slides.

Some contingencies

This is a Simulation Game, a small segment of reality. Do not attempt to make every factor of the game fit a real situation. To assist your playing of the game, consider the following:

1. You do have a personal copy of the Good News Bible.
2. You will be teaching the class for an indefinite period of time.
3. You can choose the age group of your class.
4. For the purposes of the game, the resources will be available only if they are delivered to you. (You cannot depend upon gathering a box of old magazines from the neighbours.)
5. Do not consider how large the items are or how much they weigh.
6. For items like filmstrips, records, and materials for creative activities, you can choose which titles or materials you would want to have.

Next step

Rank the items listed on the worksheet by yourself. You are then informed that two other people are going to work with you in teaching the class. It just so happens that these people are with you at the time of the phone call. Now they must participate with you in deciding on one priority list of the resources you need in order to teach.

Work with two or three other people. You have fifteen minutes in which to arrive at a priority list for your group. Some suggestions that may help:
○ Decide which age group you are going to be working with.
○ Avoid decisions based on a mathematical average.
○ Consider the reasons why another person has ranked items high or low.
○ Be flexible and willing to change.
○ And be positive about your rationale for ranking the items as you did.

After playing the game

Reflection and discussion

Here are some ideas and suggestions for the leader of the session as he guides the group in a period of reflection and discussion. The primary values of using the game in a training event are derived from the interaction of the group members with each other, with the leader, and with the game.

When all the groups have finished deciding on their priority lists, plan twenty to thirty minutes for discussion. As groups are finishing at different times, this is

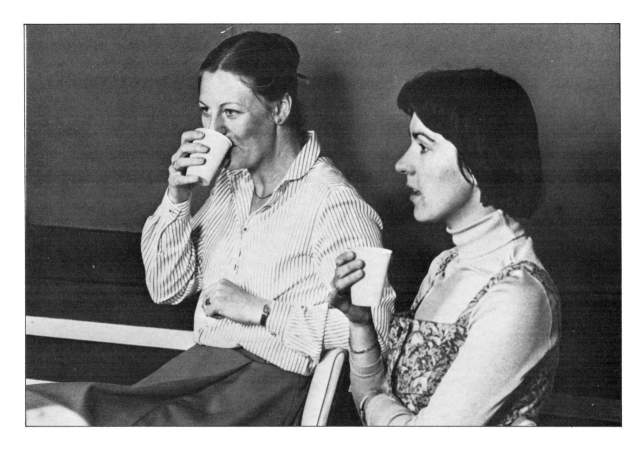

a good place for a coffee break. Also, tabulate each group's rankings on a large chart, an overhead transparency, or a blackboard.

The first question to consider is: "What were the factors that influenced the decisions you made when you were ranking the items by yourself?"

There will be a variety of responses:

1. **Age** of the students

Some items will be more appropriate for one age group than another. For instance: Bible Atlas, Dictionary, and Encyclopaedia may not be high priority for teachers of younger children.

2. **Needs** of the teacher

Items such as teaching manuals and ideas books may be ranked high by persons feeling the need for suggestions, outlines, or plans for teaching.

3. **Versatility** of resources

A tape recorder, with blank tapes, provides more flexibility in classroom use than a record player. A box of old magazines can be used in a wide variety of ways; whereas a set of teaching pictures or posters may be more limiting. With old magazines a teacher can create his own posters or teaching pictures.

4. **Usefulness** to the students

Resources such as the creative activities kit, tape recorder, old magazines and *Good News Bible* can be used by the students in pursuing and expressing their own learning and interests. These allow for considerable involvement by the students.

5. **Skills** of the teacher

A teacher who has no skill in reading music or leading singing is not likely to place a hymnbook high on his priority list. Also, a teacher with considerable skill in music may not place a hymnbook high because of his ability to teach songs and lead singing without one. Other items may suggest similar responses by teachers with different skills.

6. **Experience** of the teacher

Some teachers have had wide experience with specific resources and have discovered their value in teaching. If a teacher has often used a tape recorder in his teaching, and experienced success, he is likely to place it high on his priority list. With the same reasoning a person who has never used a tape recorder is likely to place it low.

We have considered six factors which may have influenced a person as he was ranking the items on the list in order of priority. Many other factors may emerge in the discussion.

Implications for planning

These factors influence teachers all the time. When teachers approach their planning of specific lessons, they either use or disregard suggestions from books or other people, and then add their own ideas according to their conscious or unconscious consideration of many of the factors just mentioned. Consider briefly the situation of team-teaching in a particular class. When two or more people are together they bring with them to their planning and teaching different experiences, needs, skills, attitudes, and approaches to teaching. Many breakdowns in the team-teaching process are a result of people assuming that others share the same points of view when in fact they may have very different ideas.

Perhaps participating in a process of decision-making and discussion similar to the Teacher Survival Simulation Game would help people to focus on their own individual skills and needs. When facing these differences at the beginning of their teaching together, it may be possible for them to come to a mutual understanding of each one's place and potential in the planning and teaching process. Often when people discuss the reasons for making their choices in the Simulation Game, they discover something from the other people that influences them so that they adjust the way they have ranked certain items.

Using the Teacher Survival Game in teacher education

By participating in the Teacher Survival Simulation Game, people are helped to:

1. Consider a wider variety of resources for teaching rather than limiting themselves to the items that they are used to.
2. Consider the value of one item against another as they select which items to have.
3. Hear the values placed on some resources by people with different skills, interests, and needs.
4. Participate in the process of decision-making and priority-setting with others who may share similar as well as different points of view.

The game can be used successfully as the initial training experience of a new group or staff of teachers. By using the game, people are involved immediately in the process. The task of ranking the twelve items can be easily accomplished by both experienced and inexperienced teachers.

As a result of making decisions and discussing their implications, teachers quickly face some of the key factors involved in planning and teaching. The experience of playing *Teacher Survival* can be followed by a series of training events that focus more specifically on the procedures of planning, the implementation of resources, the skills of classroom interaction and the content of teaching sessions.

Local users of the game should experiment with developing their own resource lists. Included might be items readily available in a given church or locality — or they might be items that a planning group hopes to introduce to the players.

The Recycle Game

This game was first designed for use in a teacher training event. However, as the concept of recycling resources is so important for teachers to consider, it is suggested that if you are reading this book by yourself you plan for a time when you could play this game, or parts of it, with three or more people whom you have invited to meet with you.

For a long time people have been recycling available resources for teaching in the church. When Jesus focused the attention of the people on sheep, a father and two sons, a house built on rock and other familiar objects he was recycling common, available resources to communicate something of what he understood about life, man and God. To recycle something is to use it over again in a new way to serve other purposes than those for which it was originally intended.

Recycling is an "in" process these days, with emphasis on saving the environment. The more I consider the concept of recycling and try recycling some resources myself, the more I become convinced that teachers in the church need to develop an attitude of mind that encourages them to employ the recycling process in their planning for teaching. As a result of this interest I have developed a workshop design that introduces teachers to the experience of recycling.

Step One

Introduce the concept of recycling with some examples and illustrations.

Step Two

Distribute any articles or magazines you can find that deal with the idea of recycling.

Step Three

Divide the large group into smaller groups of three to six people. Give each group one of the following items, or let them select one of the items for themselves:

○ a bowl of mixed fruit
○ a loaf of bread (unsliced)
○ a jug of cold water
○ a bag of mixed sweets
○ a package of food like biscuits, cereal, crackers, crisps
○ a bowl or bag of nuts

Allow the groups fifteen minutes to decide on one or more ways their "resource" could be used to help students focus on a biblical-theological concept.

Groups should prepare to present their ideas as quickly as possible. Spend as much time as necessary to hear from each group. Also, the groups may want to involve the others in experiencing what they have planned.

Use the food as a part of the refreshment break.

Step Four

Repeat the above process, only with different items which could include:

○ a children's game
○ a child's toy
○ a magazine

- ○ a newspaper
- ○ a football
- ○ a wallet or purse
- ○ some empty cartons of various sizes
- ○ a suitcase
- ○ a mail-order catalogue
- ○ wrist watch or alarm clock

In this period people should have up to half an hour to prepare a way to use the resource as part of a larger strategy for a classroom session.

If a spirit duplicator is available, it is very helpful to the whole group for the small groups to write up their strategy on a spirit master to duplicate and distribute to everyone present. In this way each person will be able to take home with him as many plans as there are groups.

Step Five

Distribute copies of the *Good News Bible*. Have a few Concordances available also.

Instruct people to spend five to ten minutes locating a verse or passage of scripture that illustrates the concept of recycling. Each person shares his passage with the whole group or a smaller group.

Step Six

This is the closing experience of the workshop. Encourage people to complete the statement, "Recycling is . . ." These statements then become the parts of a litany. To each of the statements the whole group could respond with "Thank you, God, for your creative spirit."

Gimmicks and Gadgets versus creative use of resources

Teachers are as much a target for educational marketing specialists as children are for the toy manufacturers. There is always something new being promoted as the newest, best, easiest to use, most successful or whatever. In our desire to motivate students and to increase our effectiveness it is not surprising that we are sold the latest gadget or gimmick. (I have a cupboard full of such purchases.) But, we need to keep in mind several concerns as we consider buying or using a new resource, technique, or piece of equipment:

1. Will I be able to use it (the resource, technique, or equipment) more than once? We do not have enough money to be able to afford one-time use of anything. It is much more valuable if it can be used several times in a variety of ways.

2. Does it supplement the curriculum I am using or do I have to dispense with my curriculum? A resource is much more valuable if I can use it to supplement the given curriculum.

3. Is the resource primarily for me or for the student? Ordinarily the resource is worth more if it is something that engages the student's interest and involvement. I need some resources too, but if I have to choose between something for me or something for the students I will seldom be wrong if I choose in the student's favour.

4. Does the resource come with a manual, user's guide, or outline of suggested uses? I can be sure the resource will be used more often and more effectively if the producers, authors, or manufacturers have offered a helpful list of practical, easy to use suggestions or procedures.

5. Does the resource encourage student exploration, involvement and creativity? If students can remain passive when using the resource then it is not as valuable as when students must be actively engaged with the resource.

By considering these questions and others we may be able to avoid being sold a gadget or gimmick that looks attractive and promising but ends up being just another disappointment. When we carefully assess the value of a new resource, technique, or piece of equipment and consider the many ways it can be used effectively as part of our teaching then it becomes a very valuable creative resource that is worth whatever it costs.

It is not a question of whether to use media or not, but rather *which* medium or media. A lecture is one type of medium and a field trip is another. Reading about Jerusalem is a medium using the printed word, seeing a filmstrip or movie showing Jerusalem is a visual medium, and interviewing a person who has visited Jerusalem is a more personalized way of discovering Jerusalem.

Teachers are the most valuable resource

When we have budgeted money for church education, built classrooms, purchased equipment, selected a curriculum and arranged for a schedule we have contributed much to creating an effective church education programme. However, the most valuable resource for teaching has not been mentioned yet — the teacher. It doesn't make much difference which curriculum, how many filmstrips, or how many square feet of floor space per student we have, if we have not recognized that the most critical factor determining the success of Christian education is the teacher. Teachers do what no curriculum or media resource will ever be able to do — smile, laugh, relate, show interest and surprise, love, forgive, touch, cry, pray, shout, whisper and so many other human responses.

7 Practise the Planning Process

In the previous four chapters we have discussed four of the essential components of the planning process.

First, we considered the key concepts to be focused upon in a session or unit of study. This is one way to respond to the question "What am I going to teach?"

Second, we compared the differences between general goals and specific instructional objectives, concluding that determining objectives for teaching is crucial to the planning process. This is a way to answer the question "What will the students learn?"

Third, we focused on four different levels of teaching activities with the observation that there are many different activities that can be selected for involving students in learning. In this chapter we responded to the question "What teaching activities will I plan for the session?"

Fourth, we identified a wide variety of resources that are available that can be used by teachers and students to make teaching and learning a very involving and interesting experience. The question "What resources will we use?" was considered in this chapter.

When you put it all together it is like building a bridge.

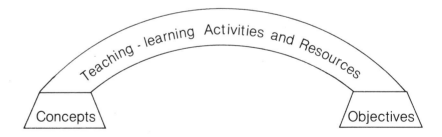

The teaching activities and resources will be just "busy-work" if they are not directly connected to the concepts we want to communicate and the objectives we want to achieve.

In order to put into practice this process of planning, teachers are encouraged to use the materials on the following pages. There are instructions for each step, and a worksheet is provided on page 50. It works best if you can do this activity with at least one other person. The instructions suggest that you plan for just one session. However, if you have time you may want to plan for two or three more sessions to complete a unit of study.

Introduction

Practise the planning process

You are a teacher of a class of students. Determine for yourself the age of your students. You meet with your class for one hour each week. Next week's lesson begins a new unit on **Jesus' Disciples, Then and Now.** Below you will find a lot of suggestions that you could use in your teaching. You cannot teach everything. You must start somewhere. So, select what you want to teach in your first session.

Step One

Select the **main ideas** you want to focus on in Session One. **Write them on the worksheet.** (See page 50.)

A. Jesus called twelve men to become his apostles.

B. Other people who learned from Jesus and followed him were called disciples.

C. A disciple is a person who follows and learns from someone else. The word is used in the New Testament of the followers of John the Baptist and Paul, but especially of the followers of Jesus.

D. Peter, Andrew, James, John, Thomas, Matthew, Judas, and five other men were the twelve apostles.

E. The apostles continued Jesus' ministry after his death.

F. In the Book of the Acts of the Apostles there are many accounts of the work the apostles did to establish the Church.

G. The apostles had difficulties in understanding Jesus' work and teachings and many times asked him questions, were unfaithful in their following, or argued among themselves.

H. The apostles were very enthusiastic about and committed to the work Jesus called them to do and many times spoke and acted fearlessly.

I. Jesus needs disciples to serve him today by speaking and acting in the world to bring love, peace, justice and health to mankind.

J. There are people today who are acting like the disciples in the early church.

K. The problems and circumstances of today are in many ways similar to those in the days of the first disciples.

L. (Write your own.)

Step Two

Select the **objectives** that are appropriate for the main ideas you have already selected. **Write them on the worksheet.**

At the end of the session the students should be able to:

A. **Define** in their own words the meaning of disciple, apostle, called, learn, and follow.

B. **Name** the twelve apostles chosen by Jesus.

C. **Identify** four of the apostles and **describe** several important characteristics or actions of each.

D. **Explain** the difference between disciple and apostle.

E. **Locate** three places in the New Testament where the twelve apostles are listed.

F. **Locate** at least six passages of scripture that **describe** some of the actions of the apostles and disciples.

G. **Describe** some of the problems the disciples had in following Jesus.

H. **Identify** with the feelings the disciples had when they learned that Jesus was crucified.

I. **Suggest** some examples of ways people are speaking and acting today as disciples.

J. **Apply** the meaning of discipleship in the New Testament to the needs of the world today.

K. **Decide** on several ways they can be disciples in their homes, school, and neighbourhood.

L. (Write your own.)

Step Three

Select **teaching activities** that will help communicate the main ideas and achieve the objectives. Select at least one activity for each of the five parts of the session: Opening, Presenting, Exploring, Creating, and Concluding. **Write them on your worksheet.**

A. Ask questions about key concepts and do research in the New Testament and other resource books.

B. Investigate one or more key people by reading key passages of scripture and other resource books.

C. See a filmstrip on the twelve apostles and look for important events, relationships with Jesus, and/or personal experiences and characteristics.

D. Write a script for a filmstrip about the apostles of Jesus.

E. Create slides to illustrate a story about Jesus and the disciples.

F. Listen to or read a story about Jesus and his disciples in his day; and in our day.

G. Write a story about experiences people have in trying to be followers of Jesus.

H. Search in magazines or newspapers to find examples of modern disciples of Jesus.

I. Work on a values clarification strategy, using rank order or voting to focus on disciples and discipleship (see chapter 11).

J. Use magazines to make a collage or montage, to mount teaching pictures, to photograph for slides, or to do picture lifting for slides or transparencies.

K. Do some informal role play or dramatics.

L. Discuss some situations where disciples are needed today and decide ways to act as disciples.

M. (Make up your own activities.)

Step Four

Select **resources** that are necessary to do the activities that are planned. **Write your own choices on the worksheet.**

A. Copies of the New Testament for each student.

B. A Bible Dictionary, Encyclopaedia, Concordance, Commentary and Atlas, several copies of each if possible.

C. A filmstrip about the followers of Jesus, then or now.

D. Overhead projector with all necessary materials and screen.

E. Cassette tape recorder with mains lead, microphone, and blank tapes.

F. Write-on slides or write-on filmstrip material with suitable pens and pencils.

G. Box of newspapers and magazines, scissors, glue, and construction paper.

H. Blank paper and felt pens or pencils.

I. Pre-recorded cassette about being a disciple.

J. A set of teaching pictures on Jesus and the apostles.

K. Materials to create puppets.

L. (Make up your own resources.)

Planning for teaching
Worksheet

Main Ideas for Session One

Instructional Objectives for Session One
At the end of the session the students should be able to:

Time	Teaching Activities	Resources
Opening		
Presenting		
Exploring		
Responding creatively		
Concluding		

A Sample Lesson Plan

There are many ways to plan for teaching. Compare this lesson plan with the one you have just made. Use the criteria outlined in the next chapter to evaluate both your plan and this sample plan. Compare the similarities and differences between the two plans.

Main Idea

People are called by Jesus to become his disciples. Twelve of Jesus' original disciples were identified as Apostles. The twelve apostles followed and learned from Jesus. Each of the twelve apostles was unique.

Instructional objectives

At the end of the session the students should be able to:

1. Define disciple and apostle in their own words.
2. Find three places where the twelve apostles are listed.
3. Describe some unique characteristics and actions of one apostle.
4. Express in whichever way they choose their own idea of one apostle and the ways in which they identify with that apostle.

Time	Teaching Activities	Resources
Opening 5 minutes	Students read definitions of disciple and apostle in the *Good News Bible* Word List and a Bible Dictionary. List various endings to these sentences: "A disciple is . . ." "An apostle is . . ."	Good News Bible Bible Dictionary Bible Encyclopaedia
Presenting the subject 10 minutes	Ask the question: "Who were the 12 disciples specially chosen by Jesus?" Write names down. Accept all names suggested. Evaluate later. Use the *Good News Bible* Index to find lists of disciples' names in three gospels. Compare with original suggestions. Compare the three lists and discuss similarities and differences. (Prepare the lists before the session to save time.)	 Newsprint and felt markers Good News Bibles Pre-prepared copies of the three lists.

Time	Teaching Activities	Resources
Exploring the subject 15 minutes	Select one disciple and use various resources to explore using some of these questions: 1. What does the disciple's name mean? 2. How did he first meet Jesus? 3. What are some special things he did? 4. What kind of a person was he? 5. What kind of relationship did he have with Jesus?	Dictionary of Bible People Bible Dictionaries Bible Encyclopaedia Chart with questions
Responding creatively 15 minutes	Students select one of the three activities to express what they have learnt about and their impressions of the disciple they have investigated. 1. Write a brief letter introducing yourself as a disciple. Write the letter in the first person, in the role of the disciple. 2. Create a set of write-on slides to illustrate some of the memorable characteristics of your disciple or some of the important events in his life. 3. Work with another student, using a tape recorder to create and record an interview with your disciple.	Paper and pencils Write-on slides, pens, pencils and projector Cassette tape recorder
Concluding 10 minutes	Share letters, slides and recordings with the whole class. Last activity: Complete the sentence, ''Disciples are . . .'' Use completed sentences as parts of a Litany. A corporate response could be: ''Help us, God, to follow Jesus and to serve others.''	

8

Criteria for Evaluating Lesson Plans

After you have created your practice lesson plan or any other lesson plan you intend to use with your students you could use the following criteria as a basis for evaluating the plans. In the list of criteria you will first read a question that should be asked of your lesson plan, then there is a brief commentary on that question to help you in your evaluation. Also included is a reference to another chapter in this manual where you will find further discussion of the principles and skills implied by the question and commentary.

1. *Is the main idea limited to a few key concepts?*
One of the important aspects of planning for teaching is to limit the number of concepts to be communicated in one session. It is possible for the *teacher* to "cover" a lot of concepts in one session, but it is much more important for the *students* to participate in "uncovering" a few key concepts. Keep the concepts connected to each other and related to the students' own experiences.

For review of this subject read again chapter three, *Focus on Key Concepts.*

2. *Are the main ideas and objectives appropriate for the age group?*
With younger students it is more important to select appropriate parts of a story or event than it is to try to teach the whole story. We need to be sure the students have mastered some of the basic skills before expecting them to achieve more complex objectives. With older students we can deal with abstractions and symbols whereas younger students will be more limited by their concrete thinking.

For review of this subject look over chapters three and four, *Focus on Key Concepts* and *Focus on Instructional Objectives.*

3. *Are the main ideas and objectives directly connected?*
It is not surprising to find situations where main ideas and objectives are not directly related to each other. For instance, teachers often select a main idea related to slavery of the Hebrews in Egypt and then select an objective focusing on contemporary forms and situations of slavery.

Slavery is the only thing connecting the two, but the historical situations are three thousand years apart. If the main idea of the Hebrews as slaves in Egypt is introduced then the objective should be related to the main idea and not to contemporary forms of slavery. If that objective is intended then a related main idea should be selected. It would be possible to use both main ideas and both objectives even in the same session.

4. *Which types of teaching activities and resources are to be used?*
In reviewing all the teaching activities and resources that are planned there should be a balance of verbal, visual, simulated and direct experiences. If there is a heavy use of just verbal activities and resources then the plan is out of balance. There needs to be a blending of all the different types of experiences.

Check again on chapters five and six, *Focus on Teaching-learning Activities* and *Focus on Teaching-learning Resources.*

5. *What kinds of questions did the teachers ask during the session?*
There are at least three categories of questions which include information, analytical and personal questions. All three types of questions should be asked during the session. If there are more information questions than the other two categories, then the students are not being encouraged to think enough and apply the subject matter to their own lives.

For more on the subject of question asking, turn to chapter nine, *The Art of Asking Questions.*

6. *What choices did the students have to make during the session?*
Every student should have the opportunity to make a number of choices during the sessions. Students are more motivated and more involved when they are encouraged to make choices during the session. Some choices are small, like deciding which book to read or which colours to use to express a feeling. Other choices may be big, like deciding how to interpret a passage of scripture or deciding how to act in a particular situation. Small or big, students need many opportunities to make choices.

The subject of student choices is presented in more detail in chapter twelve, *Ways to Increase Student Participation.*

7. *Are there a variety of activities and resources planned for the session?*
A one activity lesson is a dull lesson. Students have different abilities, interests and needs so that teachers must plan for a variety of activities and resources in order to respond to the differences between individual students. Students need a change of pace, they need to build from one activity to the next in order to maintain a high level of motivation.

Read further in chapters ten and twelve, *Creative Uses of Media* and *Ways to Increase Student Participation.*

8. *If the students are expected to do something new, have they had a chance to practise or experiment?*

Teachers should regularly introduce new activities and resources for the students to use in their exploring and creating. In order to ensure the student's success with new activities and resources, there needs to be a time for practice and experimentation where students can find out for themselves how to do or use what the teacher has planned. The same principle applies to the teacher who plans to use a new resource or try a new activity. There needs to be time allowed for previewing, practising and experimenting by the teacher.

9. *Has the room been arranged to facilitate the achievement of the intended objectives?*

Arrangement of tables and chairs; placing of learning centres, activity corners and resource equipment; display of visual materials on the wall, bulletin board or blackboard; and easy accessibility of all necessary supplies: all contribute significantly to the smooth functioning of the class and achievement of the intended objectives. Look at your room before the students arrive. What does the room say to you?

It should speak very loudly of what is expected to happen in that session. The room arrangement needs to be changed regularly, sometimes as often as weekly.

10. *How much time will be required for each of the planned activities?*

The best lesson plan ever can be "shot-down" if sufficient time has not been allowed for each activity. Be realistic about time. Allow enough time for students to work without being rushed. Be flexible enough to adjust the schedule if necessary. Also, plan for some additional activities for those students who work more quickly or have more ability.

By applying these questions to the plans you have made it should be possible to evaluate what you have planned before trying to teach the plan. If you can discuss the plan with someone else you should be able to receive enough feedback for your responses to the questions to be realistic. Consider reworking some of your plans before you enter the classroom to teach them.

9 The Art of Asking Questions

Some of us remember when it was said, "Children should be seen and not heard." Perhaps we also remember teachers we had who did most of the talking. Now we live in a day when we encourage children to express themselves to be heard by adults, and when teachers are aware that learning does not take place so much when teachers themselves do most of the talking. Interaction is basic to communication and learning. Interaction happens when teachers and students express themselves directly and listen to each other attentively. When I ask students to recall their favourite teachers and to reflect on what it was about those teachers that they liked, more often than not the students respond with comments like:

"They are really interested in what I think and say."

"They make the subject interesting so that you want to talk about it."

"They don't make you feel stupid when you give dumb answers."

"They really listen to me."

All of these comments demonstrate that the students truly appreciate a teacher who has developed some skills in guiding classroom interaction.

This chapter will focus on the skill of asking questions. Perhaps the most important resource for guiding student thinking and learning is **questions.** Questions are the least expensive resource available to us — they only cost the time it takes to plan for or think of them. I dare say it is no exaggeration to conclude that every teacher uses many questions every time he teaches. Questions are very flexible because they can be asked by teachers and students.

○ Teachers can ask questions to a whole class.

○ Teachers can ask a question of one student.
○ Questions can be written on worksheets or tests.
○ Questions can be used as part of a set of instructions.
○ Students can ask questions of teachers.
○ Students can ask questions of each other.
○ Students can raise questions for their own research.

In addition to the many ways that questions can be asked, it is possible to combine questions with a wide variety of teaching-learning activities and resources.

Questions can be used to:
○ stimulate a discussion of a familiar subject
○ introduce a new subject
○ review a subject studied previously
○ reflect on some personal experiences
○ connect a biblical subject to some personal experiences
○ interpret a biblical passage
○ motivate further research into a subject
○ evaluate a film, filmstrip, recording, etc
○ probe further into a subject
○ analyze a personal or social problem
○ debrief a simulation game or other activity
○ brainstorm solutions to a problem or issue
○ interview a guest resource person
○ consider possible alternative actions or individuals
○ clarify the values people express
○ explore people's beliefs and commitments

Questions come in many different shapes and sizes and can be used in many different ways. They can be categorized in several ways.

1. One educator classifies teacher's questions into four main categories.
a) **Cognitive recall** — questions which simply ask for specific facts gained from reading a book, watching a film or hearing a lecture.
Example: "What happened to Joseph after his brothers sold him to the caravan?"
b) **Convergent** — questions which utilize common information to prove a point or support a generalization.
Example: "What evidence is there that Joseph . . .?"
"How do you know that . . .?"
"Compare the actions of Joseph with . . ."

c) **Divergent** — questions which make use of some known information as a starting point, but the answer moves in another direction.
Example: "How would you feel if your brothers sold you and you were taken to a foreign country?"
"What would happen if . . .?"
d) **Evaluative** — questions which seek to use known information to reach some kind of a value judgement.
Example: "Was Joseph right in telling his brothers of the dreams he had?"

2. Another educator classifies teacher and student questions into three general categories.
a) **Big, perennial, life-destiny, open-ended questions.**
The answers to these questions involve us in continual debate. The answers must be followed with another question because there never is a final absolute answer.
Example: "Who am I?" "Who is God?" "What is faith?"
b) **Middle-sized, means-ends questions.**
There are good answers to these questions, but we should put a semi-colon after these answers to symbolize that there is more to learn, the answers are not final.
Example: "What do you value most?"
"What does it mean to you to be a Christian?"
c) **Small, questions of means.**
Important questions of limited scope seeking information, statement of fact.
Example: "Where would you look to find the meaning of the word covenant?"

3. I have chosen another way to categorize questions which I identify as the P-A-I approach. Most questions can easily be identified by one of the following three categories.
P — Personal Level of questions
These are questions that are related to a person's own life experience, questions a student can identify with personally. The intent of instruction is to guide students in their personal **decision-making** and **value-forming**. Questions at this level are an effective means of engaging students in the process of thinking, reflecting, expressing, and acting on concerns that relate to them personally.
Some examples:
"If *you* had been Moses, what would *you* have done when . . .?"
"When have *you* been asked to do something that was very hard for you to do?"

A — Analytical level of questions

Analytical questions require students to **think** in order to respond. Analytical questions do not assume right answers. Questions of this type are more open, with the potential of many different answers or responses. The same analytical question could be asked of every student in the class, with each giving a different response. Analytical questions ask, "What do you think . . .?" and suggest that the teacher really wants to know what the student thinks and will accept the student's thoughts.

Some examples:

"Why do you think Moses was reluctant to return to Egypt?"

"What do you think Moses meant when he said . . .?"

I — Information level of questions

Information questions require students to **remember something** in order to answer the question. As a result of reading, hearing, or otherwise receiving information, the students are expected to remember some of the facts. Information questions are more closed as they tend to assume that there are right answers. Students who are asked a lot of information level questions often feel they are being tested. It is almost impossible to have a discussion guided by information questions.

Some examples:

"Where did Moses live as a young child?"

"To what country did Moses flee after killing the Egyptian?"

Some General Comments

Too often teachers ask questions without having prepared them in advance. Information questions are the easiest to ask, but other than getting a right answer they do not lead very far unless they are followed up with Analytical and Personal questions. Questions are one of the primary means of motivating students to think and express themselves and thereby become more involved in learning. Teachers should plan carefully some key Analytical and Personal questions for use in the class period to pursue some of the information that is presented. A balance of questions representing all three levels will help students and teachers to experience a lot of interaction and to learn from each other.

A discovery in Hawaii

When I present these three levels of questions in a workshop, I usually start with Information questions, then move to Analytical and Personal questions. When I make the presentation I use an overhead projector and write the three key words on a transparency.

While doing a workshop in Hawaii I was struck by the three letters P-A-I and had a hunch that these letters may form an Hawaiian word. Hawaiian words have a lot of syllables and in speaking every syllable is pronounced. I suggested that this was a possibility, but no one present knew enough Hawaiian to know for sure whether or not "pai" was a word. The next day a woman returned to the workshop and presented me with a paper that had a few notes she had copied from an Hawaiian-English dictionary. Sure enough "pai" is an Hawaiian word with many possible meanings. However, the preferred translation of "pai" is: "To stir up, lift up, arouse and excite." What a discovery! Perhaps if teachers were to use a balanced mixture of Personal, Analytical, and Information questions students would really be stirred up, aroused, encouraged, and excited to think, reflect, and express themselves as they are involved in learning activities.

Practise identifying and writing three levels of questions

Step One

Read Luke 15.11-32

Step Two

Classify the following questions according to the three levels (P) Personal, (A) Analytical, (I) Information.

○ Who are the three main characters in this parable?

○ Why do you think Jesus told this parable?

○ If you had been the younger son, how would you have felt as you were walking back to your father?

○ What feelings do you think the father had when the younger son left home? When he returned home? When the older son inquired about the party?

○ What did the younger son say to himself when he decided to return to his father?

○ Think of some instances when you have been forgiven by someone. How did you feel?

○ What do you think this parable teaches us about the relationship between God and people?

Step Three

Read Matthew 18.21-35 about the Parable of the Unforgiving Servant. Write two questions to represent each level based on that parable.

Information

1.

2.

Analytical

1.

2.

Personal
1.
2.

Step Four

Compare your questions with someone else's and evaluate your questions together.

Step Five

Write questions appropriate for the next session you will be teaching.

Some helpful guidelines for asking questions

1. *Ask questions that are more open than closed.*
Questions with only one right answer or implying a "yes" or "no" response are more closed. These questions are more a test of memory than they are an inquiry into subject matter. When tempted to ask a closed question, make a statement instead. Then ask open, analytical, probing questions.

2. *Ask only one question at a time.*
More than one question is confusing to the student. Teachers who ask several questions at once usually have not thought carefully or prepared adequately and are "fishing" for the right question.

3. *Present questions to the whole class.*
Instead of putting one student "on the spot" by directing a question to him, offer the question to the whole class. By being aware of a student's readiness it is possible to recognize who wants to answer. A student can be called upon to respond without the teacher speaking a word; through eye contact, gesture with the hand, or nod of the head.

4. *Provide feedback after a student responds.*
The teacher can encourage students and facilitate further discussion by providing verbal and non-verbal feedback so that they will know the teacher has heard and understood their reply.

5. *After an initial question and reply, follow up with probing questions.*
Probing questions lead to further inquiry and exploration in depth of a subject. Probing questions can also provide a degree of reinforcement and feedback.

6. *After asking a question, be silent.*
The best "next step" after asking a question is to be silent. If the question is

clearly stated and if the students have sufficient data with which to answer, then they need some time to think. Ten seconds is not too much time. However, ten seconds of silence can feel like an eternity to a teacher who is a little anxious. Leave the burden of the silence on the students. Bite your tongue and relax; usually someone will respond.

7. *Be inquiring rather than interrogative.*
Inquiry is a style or approach that says to the student, "I'm with you; I'm interested in what you think and say." Interrogation puts people on the defensive and inhibits their ability to think and express themselves.

8. *Encourage students to ask their own questions.*
Questions are not just the property of the teacher, but can also be used effectively by the students.

9. *Avoid echoing students' replies.*
There are two reasons for repeating students' replies: to reinforce the answer or to say it loud enough so that others can hear who might have missed it the first time.

10. *Accept student replies as if they were gifts.*
When a student ventures to answer a question, he is risking something of himself. Every student hopes his answers will be accepted. Students will feel more confident to reply to open questions than to closed questions. Also, teachers will be more able to accept replies to open questions. We are not always perfectly pleased with every gift we receive, but we are usually gracious in receiving even the ones we are not pleased with.

Practise listening to your own questions

With a tape recorder and a little time there are many ways that teachers can focus on their question-asking skill and work at improving that skill. The first step is to record a portion of a class session where the teacher has planned to use questions to guide a discussion or to motivate further exploration. The next step could be any one of the following.

1. Write down all the questions you asked and categorize them according to the three categories of Information, Analytical and Personal.
2. Listen for how long a period of silence followed each question. Who broke the silence, the student or the teacher?

3. Listen for the kind of feedback that the teacher provided to the students after they had made a statement.

4. Listen for the style of question-asking: is it inquiry or interrogation?

5. Use a stop watch for a three to five minute period to measure how much time the students talked compared to how much time the teacher talked.

6. Listen for times when the teacher could have followed up with a probing question, but did not. If the teacher had thought to ask a probing question, what could it have been?

10

Creative Use of Media

We live in a day when people are exposed to a wide variety of media in the home, school, community and church. In Christian education we can no longer depend upon the traditional teaching techniques which have been over-used by many teachers:

○ just memorizing verses or facts,

○ just listening to a teacher telling the lesson,

○ just filling in the blank spaces in workbooks.

Students have become aware of multi-media, listening centres, individualized instruction, learning contracts, experiments, and many other features that are a part of the contemporary educational scene. It is very important that those involved in Christian education seek creative, effective ways to motivate students to become actively involved in the learning process.

There are some very basic presuppositions that underlie this chapter on *Creative Use of Media.*

1. *Teachers must assume responsibility for selecting or designing resources that are appropriate for their students.*

Suggested lesson pians can only be general and suggestive. Only the teacher knows the space available, the time available, the interests, needs and skills of the students, and his or her own resourcefulness. These factors must be considered carefully when planning a lesson or unit of study. Therefore, teachers must select resources and activities or must design some others that will be appropriate to the specific classroom.

2. *Some of the most effective resources and activities are the ones the teacher discovers or designs.*

Many teachers have experienced the joy and excitement of planning an activity or using resources that they have discovered for themselves Teachers are more motivated when they use their own ideas to create an activity or resource and this encourages the students to be more interested.

3. *Students learn in many ways. A few learn well with verbal activities, many learn well with visual activities, but most students learn best when verbal and visual activities are combined.*

Christian education has traditionally focused upon written and spoken *words.* It is the students who can remember easily or who can verbalize well that the teacher tends to encourage the most, and who therefore become the ones who participate the most. The students who had less ability with words were often "turned off" by Christian education. Teachers must realize that all students do not learn in the same ways; therefore it is necessary to provide a wide variety of learning activities so that all the students will be reached in one way or another.

4. *Visual compositions are just as valid as verbal compositions.*
Because Christian education has focused primarily on written and spoken language we have forgotten the value of visual expressions to communicate meaning. In past centuries of Christian history there was a time when people were unable to read the Scriptures in their own native language. In order to communicate the truth of Scripture, many visual means were employed: painting, mosaic, sculpture, tapestry, stained glass, and drama. Today it is possible that many students can be communicated with, and can themselves communicate with, these same media as well as films, filmstrips, slides, photographs, and other visual means. A visual statement by a student using a series of write-on slides is just as valid as a verbal statement by another student.

5. *Audio-visual materials and equipment are not just tools for the teacher. They are also tools for the students.*
Most people think of audio-visual aids as aids for the teacher. Today students are more and more able to use a wide variety of media to communicate with others as a response to some specific input or as a free creative expression of meaning.

6. *There are risks involved in using media equipment and resources, but the risks are worth it.*
Anyone who has ever used a film, filmstrip, or recording has had the experience of a bulb blowing, the film jamming, the adapter plug missing, or some other calamity. I once conducted a workshop for sixty teachers on the creative use of filmstrips. After a brief introduction I pulled the screen down (it was attached to the ceiling) and it came loose from its mounting and hit me square on the head. After recovering quickly the only thing I could think to say was, "That's the risk you take in using media." Then next I said, "What is the alternative?" The alternative is to avoid using media, to turn up with notes in your pocket or book in hand and *tell the students* what is important for them to learn. As far as I am concerned that is not a viable alternative. We must take the risk, even getting hit on the head, in order to use these dynamic resources to involve the students more actively.

7. *Teachers and students must experiment and practise with media in*

order to use it creatively and effectively.

Many times teachers try to use media equipment or other resources without first practising, previewing, or testing them out. If the equipment or resources do not work the way we hoped they would, it may be because we have not worked with them enough to know what to expect. The same is true when encouraging students to use or create something with media. They need the opportunity to practise and experiment in order to know how to use it to express themselves or communicate with others.

Read on to find out about a variety of ways in which to use overhead projectors, cassette recorders, filmstrips and slides.

In conducting a workshop that emphasizes media, it would be best to select just one or two media as the focus for the workshop. Teachers will be helped most if they can experience directly demonstrations of the media methods that are introduced and then have a chance to practise with the media. The suggestions listed below are just a beginning. You will know of and discover many more creative uses of media.

**Ways to
use the overhead projector**

1. Instead of a blackboard.
Teachers do not have to turn their backs to the students, thus losing contact with them, and materials written on transparencies or acetate roll can be recalled quickly for review or emphasis.

2. Teacher-prepared materials.
Teachers are able to prepare charts, assignments, outlines, etc., before the group meets. Materials can be original, traced from a book or copied from another source.

3. Student reports.

In small groups or individually, students can prepare reports, outlines or other material to share with the whole class. By use of the overlay technique, more than one report can be presented at a time if each group prepares its material on a different section of the transparencies.

4. Student creativity.

Students can use an overhead projector to express their ideas through:
- an illustrated story,
- a "movie roll" by using a roll of acetate,
- opaque collage,
- opaque puppets.

5. Map study.

The overhead projector lends itself very well to map study. By tracing a map from an Atlas, teachers can give blank maps to students so that they can mark on boundaries, routes, cities, etc. The use of overlays makes it possible to present several items on one map, possibly by asking different groups of individuals to prepare different materials.

6. Opaque puppets.

Puppets can be created by using cardboard to cut out profiles of faces or silhouettes of people or objects. By attaching the jaw of a face with a paper fastener it is possible to simulate talking.

7. Opaque collage.

Many opaque materials lend themselves to creating a collage for the overhead projector: buttons, string, rubberbands, pipe cleaners, lolly sticks, toothpicks, yarn, etc. Students can create very beautiful and expressive collages to convey a wide variety of feelings, meanings, or images.

8. Scenes with transparent and opaque figures.

By use of opaque silhouette cut-outs and transparent overlays with a coloured cellophane background, it is possible to prepare an illustrated story adding an item at a time. The effect is similar to that of a flannelgraph.

9. Projecting words of songs, Scripture, etc.

It is often helpful to project the words of songs that people are not familiar with so that they can sing more confidently.

Also, many recorded songs that are unfamiliar can be appreciated and understood better if the words are projected. The same is true for Scripture and other types of readings.

10. Enlarging materials.

Maps, charts, illustrations, etc., can be enlarged by first tracing original material on a transparency and then projecting on to newsprint, poster board, cloth, or some other material which can be cut out, mounted, or displayed in a permanent place. Use felt pens, crayons, or chalk to trace around the projected image on the particular material.

Ways to use cassette tapes and recorders

The word "cassette" comes from a French word meaning "case." In this instance we are speaking of small, plastic cases for tape recordings. A cassette tape and recorder is the ideal way to incorporate the use of recorded resources and activities in the classroom.

Somebody once said: "Cassette recorders and tapes are the teacher's . . .
○ personal, pocket-sized radio station,
○ personal, portable university classroom,
○ audio magazine or journal,
○ personal recording studio."

The use of cassette tapes can be classified in the following categories:
○ Teacher-prepared tapes for instructional use.
○ Student-prepared tapes for response and expression.
○ Data-collecting about student participation.
○ Evaluation of classroom activities.
○ Commercially prepared tapes.

Recently a group of six teachers participated for thirty minutes in a brainstorm session on all the possible ways they could imagine for using a tape-recorder in the classroom. They came up with fifty-nine different applications. Some of these are included here.

Teacher-prepared tapes for instructional use.
1. A teacher can divide a class into smaller groups by putting directions and other items on a tape and encouraging groups of three to six students to work independently, with the tape-recorder serving as the "facilitator" of the learning activities. for example:
○ Pre-recorded instructions for a specific sequence of learning activities. Paper, pencils, worksheets, books, photographs, or other materials could be provided and incorporated into the activity. When giving instruction verbally, repeat them and then allow time for everyone to do what is expected. (Be sure at least one student knows how to operate the tape recorder.)
○ Pre-recorded stories without endings, or situations unresolved, which require students to listen, think, discuss, and respond in some way. By using a few young friends in your neighbourhood you could dramatize the stories with a variety of young voices.

2. Often teachers are unhappy with the printed or recorded scripts of filmstrips. It is possible to edit or rewrite the script, record it and have available one's own script for use with the class.

3. Some teachers are not skilled in singing or playing a piano to guide student singing. A pianist or the church choir could record some songs for the teacher to use when introducing musical activities to the class.

Student-prepared tapes.

1. Individuals or small groups of students can write scripts for already prepared filmstrips, or for their own handmade filmstrips or slide sets. After writing the script it could be recorded to accompany the visuals when presented to the rest of the class.

2. Some students who have difficulty writing stories, reports, or other written items may be helped if they are able to dictate them into a tape recorder.

3. For older students a recording of a class discussion could be used for evaluation by the whole class.

4. By recording conversations with students it would be possible to collect a variety of responses on a specific subject to use with parent groups or in teaching training.

5. The teacher could save a tape which was recorded early in the year to compare with another tape made towards the end of the year to see if any changes have occurred.

6. In teacher training people often make assumptions of what are the typical characteristics of various age groups of students. By recording a number of conversations or interviews with individual students of a specific age group it would be possible to collect a variety of responses that would reflect the spectrum of typical concepts, thoughts, expressions, or interests of that age group.

Commercially prepared tapes.

There are many producers of cassette tapes in the religious and secular education field. Some are intended for classroom use while others are designed primarily for teacher education.

1. Many record shops have a wide selection of cassette tapes of recorded music. Recorded songs or instrumental music can be used in several ways:

○ As background music while students are arriving or perhaps during a creative activity period.

○ To introduce a new song for students to learn to sing and then to sing-along with the recording.

○ To illustrate with slides, photographs, or transparencies and present as a multi-media show.

○ To focus on a specific concept or concern and use as illustration, motivation for creativity, or inspiration for reflection.

2. Bible Society has produced a recording of the *Good News Bible* New Testament and Psalms on cassette tapes. The recorded Scriptures can be used:

○ as a script for a filmstrip or slide set,

○ for small group listening,

○ by teachers at home for leisure-time listening.

Ways to use filmstrips

1. Present information to introduce a concept or an event. Show the whole

filmstrip or just part of it. The filmstrip could be shown to the whole class or individuals, or small groups could see it in a learning centre.

2. Teacher can use the filmstrip and write his own script. This would be done for several reasons:

○ the script was intended for a different age group.
○ the script was inadequate, out of date or too long.
○ the teacher has particular objectives to accomplish.

3. Students can work in a small group to select frames for which they would write their own script. This could be done even if they have not previously seen the filmstrip and heard the script. The students could then record their script with a cassette recorder.

4. Students can watch the filmstrip without the script and write captions for frames selected by the teacher. This is especially effective if the students identify with a character in the filmstrip and write their captions in the first person. Watch the filmstrip a second time with students sharing their captions.

5. Show a filmstrip to focus on specific characters so that students can identify with the people in order to participate in a follow-up role-play activity.

6. Teacher and students can watch the filmstrip without the script, and discuss selected frames while they are being shown.

7. Stop the filmstrip in the middle and discuss possible endings before showing the rest of the filmstrip.

8. Show the filmstrip in order to set the stage and motivate students for a follow-up activity.

9. Project two filmstrips on the same subject simultaneously or project a filmstrip with another medium such as slides, 16mm film, or student-created filmstrip.

10. Use write-on filmstrip material for students to create their own visuals to accompany the script.

Ways to use slides

1. Give each student four or five write-on slides to create his own story or message in response to the concept they have been discussing.

2. Students could work in small groups to create stories that include 15 to 20 frames.

3. Teachers could give students a script from a filmstrip they have seen and encourage students to create their own slides to accompany the script.

4. Using any of the slide formats (write-on, picture lift, camera-produced), students could illustrate a song, poem, or passage of Scripture.

5. Teachers could use write-on slides to present new words, visual illustrations of difficult concepts, symbols, stories, etc.

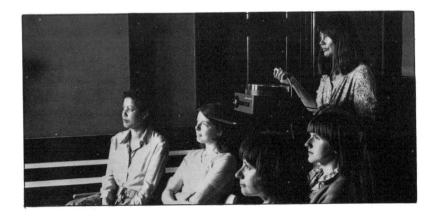

6. If two projectors and screens are available, camera-produced slides could be projected on one screen and handmade slides projected on the other screen.

7. Given a page of twenty photo slides (camera-produced) and two blank write-on slides, students could select four photo slides that have something in common with each other or that communicate a message. Then use the write-on slides as title slides to tie together the other four slides.

8. One key word, saying, sentence, or verse could be selected as the primary focus. Each person then creates one slide (from any format) to express the meaning of that statement as he ''sees'' it. All of the group's slides are then shown without comment to express the variety of meanings of the single concept.

9. Write-on slides or scratched slides lend themselves to illustrating familiar symbols or designing new ones.

10. Try creating a litany with slides instead of just verbal statements. Each student could create his own visual statement. When all slides are collected, the teacher or students can decide on a verbal response. Then project slides one at a time with the whole group responding verbally after each slide.

11. Because they are transparent, write-on slides can be placed over cartoons, line drawings, or other simple designs and the figures traced on to the slide.

12. Each person could create his own slide or slides which say something special about himself. Then as the slides are projected, each person can introduce himself by interpreting his slide.

13. For prayer, have people write or symbolize a problem, need, or person as a focus for prayer. With projector and slides it is possible to have a silent, visual prayer. Try this with appropriate background music.

14. Select and place at random 80 to 100 slides in a tray, then project and advance them in time to music or other recorded material. It is surprising how often a series of provocative slides applies to any given material without pre-arranging the order of the slides. Use the same process with two projectors and screens for double the effect.

15. Students can pose a scene, or design posters or sets, and then photograph them to tell their own story of any historical event or biblical happening they may choose. By first writing, and then recording their own script, students can create a very significant slide set to share with other classes, parents, or other groups.

There are many other ways to use these media. It is also possible to use 16mm films. See *Using the Bible with Audio-Visuals* for further details and media ideas.

Focus on criteria for selecting and using media

With many types of media available, from magazine photos to video-tape equipment, and with the large quantity of resources within each type of media, it is important that Christian educators begin to develop a set of criteria that they can use to determine the value and usefulness of various media. It is not enough to judge material solely on the basis of personal preference or taste or even on someone else's recommendation. The following list is not intended to be comprehensive, but rather to suggest some important areas for consideration.

1. Does the resource open up a subject by presenting basic information clearly, objectively, and interestingly?

2. Does the resource focus upon significant questions or issues, which people must consider seriously?

3. Are there direct or indirect connections between the subject of the resource and the essence of the Christian Gospel?

4. Does the resource invite students to think, reflect, imagine and respond with all their creative ability and insight?

5. Are the students encouraged to discuss, explore, research, or act further?

6. Can the resource be used in more than one way or in more than one situation?

7. Are there guidelines or other resources which will help the teacher use the material to the best advantage?

8. Is the resource appropriate to the age group for which it is intended?

9. If the resource is new, then time should be provided to preview or experiment.

10. The resource should not be so familiar that the students will be bored by its use.

11. The resource should not be so novel that it calls attention to itself causing its value to be lost.

12. The resource should be enjoyable and provide the students with a sense of satisfaction or accomplishment as they use it or see it being used.

By applying these criteria to a specific media resource it should be possible to determine whether or not it is worth using or buying that particular resource. If a resource gets a negative response to several of these criteria, then its purchase or use should be reconsidered.

11 Values and Teaching in Christian Education

In *Using the Bible in Teaching* (chapter nine), I have outlined the work of Dr. Sidney Simon and his colleagues from the University of Massachusetts on **value clarification.** In this chapter I shall, once again, outline the basic concepts underlying the process of values clarification, and then present a design for a workshop on values and teaching in Christian education (see page 77).

Presuppositions

1. Most Christian leaders, ministers and parents have traditionally communicated values by **moralizing.**

To moralize on values for a young person is for an older person to imply by his behaviour and statements, "I have lived long enough to have gained enough experience and wisdom to know what is right for you. Listen to me and do what I say and everything will be all right." This approach works in societies where there is a generally agreed upon consensus of what is "right", but in a society like ours with so many divergent and competing values it is not always easy to know what is right for oneself let alone for someone else. When an adult is imposing his values upon a younger person it is not helping him to become an independent, responsible, mature decision-maker.

There is another problem associated with the moralizing approach and that revolves around what is called **hypocrisy.** Hypocrisy manifests itself when the adult says, "Do what I say, not what I do." Also, hypocrisy is evident when a younger person behaves according to his own set of values when he is not in the presence of or under the authority of the adult, even though he may have assented to the adult's values in their presence.

2. In the absence of a commonly accepted set of values, some adults take a **laissez-faire approach.**

What the adult is saying to the younger person is, "Everything is all mixed up. I'm not sure what is right or wrong. Experience is the best teacher. You are on your own when finding out and deciding what is right for you. Good luck." This approach is not very helpful either. It provides no guidelines for young people as they search for what is of value.

3. Another influence on value formation is the "hero" or the "model" that a person admires.

Most young people and many adults have a variety of heroes that they admire in sports, politics, religion, films, T.V., etc. Many people's values are directly related to the values that they see in their heroes. The problem with this approach to value formation is that the hero sooner or later falls off his pedestal.

The hero is fallible and is unable to fulfil all the unrealistic expectations of the devotee.

4. **Values clarification** is a very helpful alternative to the above three approaches to the formation of values.

There are several basic characteristics and principles associated with values clarification:

○ The individual is primarily responsible for the choosing and acting out of his own values.

○ People are helped if teachers, parents, and others do not make judgements as they respond to their attempt to clarify their own values.

○ Teachers and parents are most helpful when they encourage the identification and evaluation of various alternative actions.

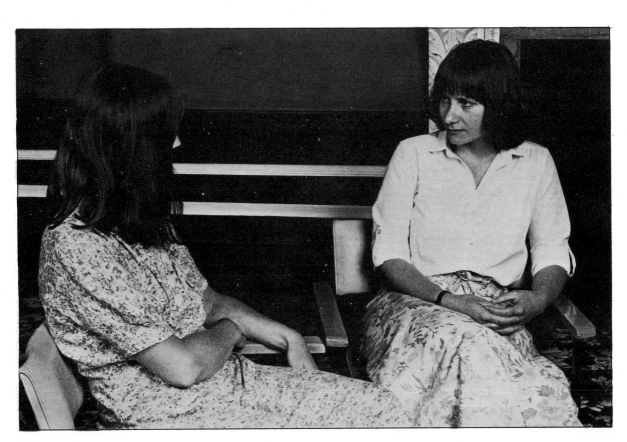

○ People need opportunities to reflect on their own values, to hear other people's values, and to affirm their own values in the presence of others.

Seven aspects of value formation

Definition

Values are those elements that show how a person has decided to use his life.

Process of Valuing

Unless something satisfies all seven of the aspects or criteria we do not call it a value.

1. **Choosing freely** — Values must be freely selected if they are to be really valued by the individual.

2. **Choosing from among alternatives** — Only when choice is possible, with more than one alternative from which to choose, do we say a value can result.

3. **Choosing after thoughtful consideration of the consequences of each alternative** — A value can emerge only with thoughtful consideration of the range of alternatives and consequences in a choice.

4. **Prizing and cherishing** — Values flow from choices we are glad to make.

5. **Affirming** — We are willing to affirm publicly our values.

6. **Acting upon choices** — For a value to be present, life itself must be affected. Nothing can be a value that does not, in fact, give direction to actual living.

7. **Repeating** — Values tend to have a persistency, tend to make a pattern in a life.

Values and value indicators

According to the seven steps identified above, many things that we have thought to be values are not really values but rather **value indicators.** Our values usually grow out of what are identified as value indicators. The following ten categories are important aspects of a person's life, but ordinarily do not fulfil all seven steps, or criteria, of value formation.

1. Goals or purposes
2. Aspirations
3. Attitudes
4. Interests
5. Feelings
6. Beliefs, convictions, ideas
7. Opinions, points of view
8. Activities
9. Worries, problems, obstacles
10. Likes or dislikes, preferences

Value-rich areas of life

All people have some values. They may not be able to articulate what their values are, but if they are making choices between alternative actions they do have values. The values clarification approach is a way to help people identify, clarify, formulate and express their own personal values.

There are some areas in our lives that are especially significant, that require us to formulate some values.

1. **Money** — how it is obtained, used, treated.

2. Friendship — how we relate to other people.

3. Love and sex — how we deal with intimate, sexual relationships.

4. Religion — what we hold as our basic beliefs.

5. Leisure — how we spend our free time.

6. Politics and social organization — who we vote for, how government is organized, what laws it passes.

7. Work — choice of vocation, time and energy spent working, attitudes towards work.

8. Family — how one behaves in relationships with parents, brothers, and sisters, children, etc.

9. Maturity — what a person strives for in order to be responsible, independent, grown-up.

10. Character traits — what people are like, the way they behave.

Here are some values clarification strategies that can be used by the teacher in Christian education. Further examples can be found in *Using the Bible in Teaching* (chapter nine).

A. Values voting

Voting is an action with which most students are familiar. Voting is fun and involves everyone. Voting requires people to make choices. Voting can set the stage for a very fruitful discussion after people have identified their positions (values) on a variety of issues. The teacher or the students could prepare the statements on which the class will vote. Each statement is prefaced by the phrase, "How many of you...?" The next word could be "think", "would", "feel", "enjoy", "are", "wish", or any one of dozens of other words that introduce the issue in a way that makes the choices personal and specific.

Some Values voting samples:

○ How many of you think that memorizing Bible verses is a good teaching activity for children?

○ How many of you would prefer to teach at church on a day other than Sunday?

○ How many of you feel that teaching in the church is a personally fulfilling experience?

○ How many of you think that the church helps people form their values more than the mass media?

○ How many of you are excited about the future potential of Christian education?

The above questions were related to the topic of teaching in the church. There are many very fruitful topics that can be used for this strategy of voting, as well as all the other strategies. These topics include: money, time, religious beliefs, politics, work, leisure, family, personal relationships, sex, school, material goods, ecology, and others.

In the voting strategy, people cast their votes by raising their hands if they agree with the statement, putting thumbs down if they disagree with it, and crossing their arms in front of them if they have no response. If they have very strong feelings, then they can wave their hands or thumbs vigorously.

B. Value clarifying responses

Value clarifying responses are very simple and natural responses from the teacher that assist students to reflect on their values. These responses can be used in any teaching situation.

1. Was that your own choice?
2. Was it a free choice?
3. What other alternatives did you consider?
4. What are some other possibilities?
5. Where would that choice lead? What would some consequences be?
6. What do you have to assume for things to work out that way?
7. How do you feel? Are you pleased with that?
8. How important is that to you?
9. Are you willing to tell others about your choice?
10. Do others know that about you?
11. Would you really do that?
12. What actions would that lead you to?

13. Would you do the same thing over again?

14. Do you do that often?

Notice that the above list includes two questions for each of the seven steps in the process of value formation.

C. The value clarifying discussion

The value clarifying discussion is a group activity. The teacher serves in the role of "facilitator" and enabler of the discussion. There are no "right" and "wrong" answers. There are many points of view. Students need to be helped to hear each other and respect their differences.

Value clarifying discussion can be initiated by:

1. Questions from Scripture or other sources.

2. Photographs, art, posters, or other sources.

3. A scene from a play.

4. A short film.

5. A tape-recorded excerpt from radio or T.V. news, talk, show, or other programme.

6. Words of a song.

7. A magazine article.

8. A Peanuts comic strip.

9. A Newspaper editorial, letters to the editor, or a Problem Page from a magazine.

10. An advertisement for a product or propaganda for a political candidate.

Questions can be formed and a discussion developed that would help students to think about and express their own personal values.

D. Rank order

Every day people make choices that reflect their priorities for their money and time, and the value they place on specific people. The priorities we establish consciously reflect the values we have. A **rank order** is a statement that introduces a situation or asks a question which is followed by three or four choices. Students are to rank the choices from highest to lowest priority. After ranking there can be time to compare and discuss the choices.

Sample rank orders:

1. If you had £20 you did not need for something else, would you:

○ buy some clothes?

○ buy some records?

○ buy some books?

2. Which do you feel Jesus would consider the greatest sin?
○ not forgiving a person who asked for forgiveness?
○ ignoring a person who needed help?
○ ridiculing another person?
3. If you could spend a day with anyone now living, who would you choose?
○ the Prime Minister?
○ your favourite sports hero or heroine?
○ a television star?
4. If you had the time, money, and skill to help solve society's problems, which would you work on?
○ saving the environment?
○ reducing the birth rate?
○ improving the education system?

**Practise
creating your own rank orders**

(Also involve students in creating rank orders.)
1. Create some on any subjects of personal interest.
2. Create some using Jesus and his teachings as the subject.

E. Alternative action search

Often people behave in one way and later, after some reflection, they wish they had acted differently. Usually there are several alternative actions that are possible in any given situation. People are helped when they can identify a variety of alternative actions that are possible, then select the one that they prefer. "Alternative action search" is a strategy in which the teacher presents in written or spoken form a situation story that is open-ended, with many possible alternative actions. The task of the students is to search for the action they would prefer to take.

Here is an example:

The situation
"You have been sent by your mother to get a prescription from the chemist. Your sister is very ill and needs the medicine right away. Your best friend sees you leaving on your bike and asks to go with you. You say O.K. On the way you see a car hit a dog that was running across the street. The car keeps on going, but the dog is lying beside the road. The dog is bleeding, but still alive. What would you do?

Instructions
1. With two or three other people, make a list of all the possible actions you and

your friend could take in response to this situation.

2. By yourself, select which actions you think you would consider doing.
3. Which *one* of these actions would *you* do? Why?
4. Compare your choice with that of the others and discuss the reasons for your choice.

Teachers can create their own alternative action search situations to focus on the concepts they seek to emphasize in a given class session.

F. A values sheet

A values sheet is something that teachers can prepare for students to work on individually or in small groups. A values sheet is a list of thought-provoking questions based upon a statement, story, question, issue, or event that causes people to make choices that reflect on their values. An example can be found in *Using the Bible in Teaching* (chapter nine).

G. A simulation game: Something of value.

Objectives

At the end of the simulation game, students will be able to:

1. Identify the values most important to them as individuals.
2. Compare their own order of personal values with that of other people.
3. Develop a sense of identity with others who have similar values.

Setting

Something of value can be played with 20-50 people. Less than 20 people will reduce the possibilities for interaction between individuals and small groups.

The room should be arranged with the chairs in groups of three or four each. There should be sufficient space to allow for people to move around and for the chairs to be rearranged in groups of up to seven chairs per group.

Materials

The materials needed by each participant are five 3" x 5" cards, a sheet of blank paper and a pencil.

Procedure

Step 1

Each person takes a seat in one of the groups of three chairs. Each person is instructed to list as many items of value to them as they can think of in two minutes. Give examples of various kinds of items which may be of value: school, a special friend, a car, a favourite dress, truth, faith in God, football, T.V., family, etc.   *Time: 2 minutes.*

Step 2

After making this list, instruct each person to select their five most important items of value and rank them in order of importance. Write one value on each card. Place the number (or rank) of the value on the back of the card (1 for top value, 5 for lowest). *Time: 2 to 3 minutes.*

Step 3

When everyone has done this, the three people in each group should exchange their sets of cards. Each person reads the other's values and then ranks them according to his own order of priority placing the numbers on the back. In this process each person will have read and ranked two other people's values in addition to his own. *Time: 3 to 4 minutes.*

Step 4

Each person receives back his own set of five cards marked on the back with the other's order of priority. Each group of three should discuss amongst themselves the similarities and differences among them and the reasons for ranking them in the order they did. *Time: 5 to 8 minutes.*

Step 5

People are then instructed to find other people with similar highest values. Each person should focus on his top one or two values and by asking the other participants find others who share his most important values. Groups should be formed with a minimum of three and a maximum of six or seven people. When a group is formed they are instructed to arrange their chairs in a part of the room that will then become "their space" for the rest of the game. *Time: 5 minutes.*

Step 6

Each newly formed group then follows the following instructions:

A. Decide on a name to identify the group's values.

B. Decide on a slogan or motto to symbolize the group's values.

C. Discuss why the group's values are most important and decide on what to tell the other groups about the importance of their values and how to convince others to join them.

D. Select someone to speak for the group. *Time: 10 to 12 minutes.*

Step 7

Call the groups to order and allow each group a maximum of two minutes to make its presentation.

Step 8

After the small group presentations, allow individuals to circulate and to "evangelize" the others, seeking "converts" to their own group.

Time: 5 to 7 minutes.

Step 9

When people have had a chance to "evangelize" others, call for the groups to reassemble. Spend just a minute calling attention to the way the groups now appear. (Often there is no change in group structures, or if there is change it may be only one or two people who have shifted. Occasionally two groups decide to merge.) *Time: 3 minutes.*

Reflection and Discussion

No simulation game should be played if there is not sufficient time allowed for discussion and reflection afterwards. The purpose of a simulation game is to provide a common experience for the whole group, related to aspects of their life, and to use the game as a basis for analyzing factors which determine personal and social values.

Some possible discussion questions:

1. How did you like the game? Any reactions?
2. Are the values you selected really *your* values?
3. How did you feel when someone else ranked your values differently from how you did?
4. How did you participate in the group's process of deciding on name, slogan and spokesman?
5. Were you successful in convincing someone else to join your group and accept your group's values? Why? Why not?
6. What would you do differently if you were to play the game again?
7. Why do you think the groups did not change much?
8. What parts of our personal and social life did this experience simulate?

Leader's Role

The leader should make the directions clear, brief, and direct. Give instructions one at a time. Better to allow less time than too much. Be aware of how far the participants have got in accomplishing their tasks. Be available to restate or interpret the directions for anyone who asks questions.

The leader could enlist one or more people to assist as observers. Observe what is happening. Make notes by writing direct quotes of what is heard or exact descriptions of what is seen.

Some things for **observers** to look for:

1. How do students make their decisions?
2. How much group loyalty is there?
3. Are some students easily led or influenced by others?
4. Do some students dominate?
5. Are there any examples of mature negotiations?

6. Is there any difference between the way people act alone compared to the way they act in a group?

The **leader** can make a summary at the end of the game which could include:
1. People do have different values. It's not always a question of right or wrong but rather of what is appropriate for the individual.
2. People's values are influenced by others.
3. Negotiating as equals is more satisfactory than giving in to someone else or dominating another.
4. People need more practice in communication.
5. People need more assurance that their values are worth keeping and building upon.

Follow-up activities.
○ Some possible creative activities could include making posters, banners, collages or murals focusing on specific values.
○ A film, speaker, recording, or field trip, might be planned to gain additional insight and information related to specific values.
○ Groups could continue for several weeks working on a multi-media presentation to communicate to others in the congregation or community the meaning and significance of their chosen values.
○ The Scriptures could be searched and discussed focusing on specific values and comparing the message of the Scriptures to the contemporary situation. Several appropriate Scriptures include:
1. Joshua 24.14-28 ". . . decide today whom you will serve . . ."
2. Psalm 15 "Lord, who may enter your Temple?"
3. Micah 6 "What he requires of us is this . . ."
4. Matthew 5-7 Sermon on the Mount: many appropriate passages.
5. Matthew 16.24-26 "If anyone wants to come with me . . ."
6. Mark 12.28-34 "Which commandment is the most important of all?"
7. Romans 12 "Do not conform yourselves to the standards of this world . . ."
8. Galatians 5.16-26 "Let the Spirit direct your lives . . ."
○ Listen to radio or T.V. commercials or read ads in a magazine to determine what values are being presented. How do these values influence our own personal values?

12

Ways to Increase Student Participation

Students will feel more motivated to participate in classroom learning activities when they can make an investment in what is happening. Whenever a person has something at stake he is more interested in the outcome. Too often teachers are the only ones who have an investment and something at stake in the hour's Christian education session. Teachers need to develop ways to help students to make an investment in the session too.

One way to encourage the students to invest in their own learning is to provide as many ways as possible for them to make decisions about what and how they are going to study. When students are offered a variety of alternatives in the way of activities and resources from which they can choose, then they are likely to participate more enthusiastically.

There are many decisions students can make in an hour's class session. Some decisions are inconsequential and others are more significant, but all opportunities to make decisions contribute to the student's sense of investing in his own learning. Students who are able to make choices about what and how they will learn are more motivated than students who are told everything they will do. Students make decisions when they . . .

1. **decide** where to sit.
2. **pick** who to work with.
3. **choose** the materials with which to create something.
4. **decide** which resource books to use for research.
5. **interpret** passages of Scripture in their own way.
6. **choose** which Scripture passages to read.
7. **select** which version of the Bible they want to read.
8. **state** answers to questions in their own words.
9. **rank** items in order of priority.
10. **ask** their own questions in their own words.
11. **elect** which learning centre or activity to use.
12. **determine** which words best describe a subject.
13. **decide** for themselves which values are most important to them.
14. **resolve** how they will act in particular situations.
15. **choose** one or more items out of a number of items.
16. **judge** for themselves from various alternatives.
17. **decide** upon a role with which to identify.
18. **test** for themselves the success of several possibilities.
19. **choose** what they want to communicate through their creativity.
20. (**state** your own examples of other student choices.)

Here are more examples of strategies and activities that can be used to involve students in deciding what and how to learn.

1. Writing a learning contract

Some students have experiences in school of writing their own learning contracts with the teacher. In order to write a contract a student needs to know something of the subject matter to be studied and all the possible activities he can do to work on the subject. With this background he may be able to fill out a contract like this one.

Learning Contract

I plan to study the following subject(s):

I will use the following learning centres:

1.

2.

3.

4.

5.

I will share the results of my study by:

I will be finished by:

_____
(date)

_____
(student's name)

_____
(teacher's name)

---

2. Selecting from several activites

The teacher may arrange several learning or activity centres in the room. Each centre should have the instructions visible and all the resources necessary to do the activity. After an introduction to the subject the students could be given a list of centres from which they could choose the one they want to work in. A sample list of activities related to the study of Amos is listed below. This list of activities was prepared for a large group of older students. If you have fewer students then you will need fewer centres. A rule of thumb I follow is to plan one centre for every four or five students.

Creative Activities for Exploring about Amos

Note: Select on activity. Meet with others who have selected the same activity. Follow the brief instructions, use the available resources and work for 30 minutes to complete your assignment.

Group One: Use filmstrip and create a script.
○ Preview the filmstrip quickly.
○ Look at the filmstrip again. Discuss each frame to determine what is portrayed.
○ Work on 5 or 6 frames at a time with each person writing a caption, description or dialogue for one frame.
○ Or, as a group talk about the frames and get one person to serve as secretary and write down what is said.
○ Some frames can be omitted if necessary.
○ Prepare to present the filmstrip and script to the whole class.

Group Two: Use script and create a set of slides.
○ Read through the script quickly.
○ Decide on which frames to illustrate.
○ Use materials available to create write-on slides.
○ Some slides can present title, captions, or dialogue as well as pictures.
○ Prepare to present slides and script to the whole class.

Group Three: Use slides to create a presentation.
○ Decide on the content of the presentation: Amos song, verses of scripture, a paraphrase of Amos, etc.
○ Select slides to illustrate the chosen content.
○ Use as many slides as desired.
○ Prepare to present slides and content to the whole class.

Group Four: Create a map presentation using overhead transparencies.
○ Use an Atlas and other books with pens, pencils and transparencies to prepare a visual presentation.
○ Consider the following questions: What were the boundaries of the Northern and Southern Kingdom? Where did Amos live, work, prophesy? What were some of the key cities and places?
○ Prepare to present transparencies to the whole class.

Group Five: Create a set of posters or banners.
○ Select a statement of judgement and a statement of hope from Amos' writing.
○ Use magazines, poster paper, felt, scissors, glue, etc. to create two posters or two banners, one a statement of judgement and the other a statement of hope.
○ Prepare to share your posters or banners with the whole class.

Group Six: Write brief articles to create a two-page newspaper.
○ Consider the geographical, political, social and religious situation of Amos' day and write several brief articles in newspaper style. Use your imagination.
○ Use a variety of styles: editorial, news, letters to the editor, cartoon, society, human interest etc.,
○ Use ball point pens to write on spirit masters in order to duplicate the paper for the class.

Group Seven: Prepare for prosecution and defence of Amos.
○ Consider Amos: the times, his writing etc.
○ Prepare a list of charges against Amos.
○ Half the group write an argument for the prosecution.
○ Half the group write an argument for the defence.
○ Prepare to present your arguments to the whole class.

3. Following instructions on worksheets

Teachers could prepare one worksheet for all students to use or several worksheets from which they could choose. Whichever way there needs to be a lot of openness with alternative activities provided for. Following are two samples of worksheets.

The Apostle Peter

Some resources to use:

1. Good News Bible
Look up Peter in the Index and read some of the references.
2. Revell's Dictionary of Bible People
Dictionary of Bible People (Scripture Union)
Look up Peter in the Index and read the pages that
describe the experiences of Peter.

Some questions to answer:

1. What are some words that best describe Peter as a
person?
2. What kind of relationship did Peter have with Jesus?
3. What was Peter's importance to the early church?
4. What are some of the important actions of Peter?

Some activities to do:

1. Write a letter of recommendation for Peter to be
considered as a minister for your church.
2. Create a series of write-on slides to describe the apostle
Peter and some of his actions.
3. Write out a list of ten to fifteen Bible verses that summarize
the important aspects of Peter's life.

Who were the twelve disciples Jesus chose?

Step One: Use either of the following two books:
a Bible Dictionary or an Encyclopaedia*.
Look up the word **Disciple** and read the
definition.

Step Two: Complete the sentence in your own words: ''A
disciple is . . .''

Step Three: Find at least one place in the New Testament
where the twelve disciples are listed.
Use Bible references in one of the books or in
the index in the *Good News Bible* to find a
place where the disciples are listed.
Hint: Look under the word **Apostle** too.

The twelve disciples (apostles) were:

1.   7.
2.   8.
3.   9.
4.   10.
5.   11.
6.   12.

Step Four: To find out more about the disciples or to help
you remember their names you can choose to
do one of the following fun things.
a. Finish a crossword puzzle.
b. Use the study-scope tube — a tube containing
papers with the names and information about
the disciples.
c. Play a game of cards — Disciple Rummy:
make a set of cards with all the disciples' names
on them for the group to play rummy with.
d. A quiz about the disciples.
e. See a filmstrip.

*Choose books suitable for the age with which you are working.

4. Values clarification strategies

All values clarification strategies (see chapter eleven) require students to make choices. When using values voting, rank order, alternative action search or any one of several dozen other strategies, the students will have a chance to invest themselves in the whole process.

5. Analysing and personalizing questions

The two categories of questions presented in chapter nine which call upon students to analyse and personalize the subject matter are examples of ways students can become more involved through the kinds of questions teachers ask.

6. Creative activities

Whenever students are provided with enough input to help them think about and explore a subject they will be able to respond creatively to express some of their insights and feelings. It is important always to have available a variety of activities which will include at least one writing, one drawing, one visualizing, one construction, and one dramatizing activity. When this variety is offered, then all the students will be able to find something that suits them.

7. Simulation activities

Simulation games and other activities all require a high degree of student involvement, as they involve students in making decisions in order to identify with people, situations and events. There is a lot of interaction among students and a lot of decision-making in simulation activities. Most simulation activities require the participation of the whole class.

When students do make decisions and do participate actively or express themselves creatively, it is important that teachers encourage and reinforce the students non-verbally as well as verbally. Dr. Ned Flanders, developer of the Interaction Analysis System, has said, "The most important moment in the classroom is the moment after the student has said or done something." The importance of the moment is in what the *teacher does* in response to what the student has said or done. Everyone needs feedback from other people. We need to know what others think of what we say and do.

Students who receive encouragement, praise, and other reinforcing responses from teachers are much more motivated to participate and do more.

We all have our favourite way of responding to students. Usually we keep saying one or two phrases that are more like a mannerism than consciously chosen responses. Each of us needs to expand our repertoire of responses so that when we do say "great" it sounds as if we really mean it and it is not just a worn out response that the students hear all the time.

Consider the following list. How many of these responses do you use habitually? Which ones could you add to your repertoire with a little practice?

Twenty-Five Ways of saying "Good for You"

1. That's great!
2. Good work!
3. Thank you very much.
4. Good idea!
5. That's a good point.
6. I like that.
7. Very interesting.
8. Terrific!
9. You're on the right track.
10. Marvellous.
11. Thank you for . . .
12. Excellent work.
13. Well done!
14. You've got the right idea.
15. Nice going.
16. That's unique.
17. Keep it up!
18. Exactly.
19. That's much better.
20. What neat work!
21. Beautiful!
22. That's a good start.
23. You make it look so easy.
24. That's an interesting way of looking at it.
25. You really did a good job!

13

Designing Teacher Education Events

This chapter is written especially for ministers, church leaders and others who are responsible for recruiting, training, and providing support for church teachers. However, if you are a church teacher do read on as you may find some ideas in this chapter that you would like to share with your minister, and other church leaders or members. If you do find something that you like, why not underline it and then pass it on to someone else to think about and work on.

A. The importance of teacher education

There was a time when I thought that if I could just find the right curriculum then most of our teaching problems would be solved. However, the more I have looked at and worked with commercially produced source materials, the more I have realized that there is never one right curriculum. There are many good curricula on the market, but each has its own strong and weak points. No curriculum is perfect, but it is important that whichever one is chosen — or written by the teachers themselves — should not expect more of its teachers and students than they are capable of giving. It must also, of course, reflect the goals to be achieved by the Christian education programme. Even then, the work has only just begun.

The **most important task** for every church is to **recruit teachers** who are motivated to teach. After teachers have been recruited they must be equipped to teach by receiving training and support that will enable them to become skilful, resourceful and effective teachers. People are not necessarily "born teachers". Some may have more natural ability than others, but anyone who is keen to teach can be trained and equipped to become a more competent and confident teacher. The success of any teaching staff or educational programme in a church will be measured directly in terms of the quantity and quality of the training and support that is available to the teachers. Every establishment involved in Christian education should develop a strategy for teacher education that will provide the necessary training and support for its own teachers. The previous twelve chapters have been one attempt to focus on some of the skills that teachers need in order to become more effective. In this chapter I shall provide an outline of some things to consider when developing a strategy for teacher education. In the *Bibliography* which follows there are many additional resources that could be considered when developing an overall strategy for teacher education.

B. Some thoughts about the recruiting and support of teachers

Before training for church teachers makes any sense, there must obviously be teachers to train. Recruiting teachers is one of the most difficult and frustrating tasks in Christian education. The difficulty may be more a symptom of other problems rather than the central problem itself. If recruiting is a symptom of other problems, some of those problems may be:

1. A poor image of the role of a teacher.
2. Low priority given to education in the church.
3. Most of the congregation are not informed about the education programme.
4. The teachers' sense of isolation and neglect.
5. The high ratio of students per teacher.
6. Irregular attendance by students and little parent support.
7. Inadequate rooms, equipment, and resources.
8. Lack of time to do adequate preparation.
9. Teachers experiencing little sense of satisfaction and accomplishment.
10. Lack of professional training and support of teachers.

As long as any of the above problems are present in a church it is likely that it will continue to be difficult to recruit teachers. At all levels of the church's life there needs to be increased commitment to and support of the church teacher.

There are a variety of things that ministers, church leaders and others can do that may help to resolve some of the problems and perhaps make the task of recruiting more manageable.

1. *Instead of filling empty "slots" recruit people who have specific skills for specific tasks.*
People are often recruited to do things they are not capable of doing. Very few people feel capable of teaching biblical and theological content. However, many people have particular interests or skills such as photography, art, music, drama, story telling, etc. Why not recruit them to do the things that they are capable of, asking them to contribute their skills and share their interests with the students. In order to do this a committee or recruiter will need to get to know the interests and skills of the church members.

2. *Instead of recruiting people for an indefinite period of time, establish clear time limits, which may be as long as two or three years or as short as one unit of study or several months.*
Everybody prefers to know exactly how long he is expected to serve as a teacher. To expect everyone to teach for a year or two may eliminate some excellent teaching possibilities. A person with photographic skills may be able to

work with a team of teachers for a unit of study where his skills could be used extensively, but not for a long period. Even those who will teach for a number of years are helped if they can see a possible stopping point ahead.

3. *Instead of recruiting people to teach by themselves, develop a system of team teaching or at least team planning.*
Low morale develops when people feel trapped and isolated in a class. These feelings can be overcome when teachers are able to work with a team of one or more other teachers. Even in small classes of ten or fewer students, there are advantages in team teaching. Teachers are able to bring a wider variety of skills and interests when there are two or more in a class. Also, it is possible for one teacher to miss an occasional Sunday without disrupting the continuity of the class. Even where it is not possible to recruit teams of teachers to teach together it may be possible to develop teams of people who can *plan* together.

4. *Instead of placing people on teaching teams like "blind dates", provide for an opportunity for people to work together in training sessions or other situations where they will have an opportunity to "court" each other and to decide for themselves with whom they want to teach.*
People who are able to choose the person with whom they will teach will be more motivated to work on developing a team relationship than if they are just told which team they will be in. Often people recruit their friends to teach with them. I think we are very unfair and unrealistic when we just assign people to teach together without carefully assessing their potential problems or values.

5. *Instead of approaching people about teaching in general, a clear statement of expectations should be presented to the prospective teacher.*
Teachers will be able to evaluate themselves better if they know exactly what is expected of them. One church prepared the following list of expectations:

What do we expect of teachers?
When a person accepts the challenge and the responsibility of teaching, we understand the following to be essential for the fulfilment of the purposes and goals of Christian teaching and learning:

a. Teachers see their task as a specific response to God and the Church expressing their Christian commitment.
b. Teachers become members of teaching teams:

○ in relation to students of a particular age, taught with other teachers.

○ in working with other teachers — guidance will be provided by a senior teacher.

○ when a larger team assists and guides the teachers in their work.

c. By participating with a team of teachers and by planning ahead there will be opportunity for occasional Sundays off.

d. Teachers continue to express themselves and find inspiration for their work through the corporate worship of the congregation.

e. To do their work well teachers must:

○ first complete a teacher's basic training course.

○ participate with the teaching team in planning and preparing weekly lessons.

○ do systematic and careful planning for each class session.

○ be regular and prompt in attendance where their participation is depended upon.

Another church prepared a little booklet entitled, "Me? A Teacher?"* which introduces the teaching ministry of the church. One section of the booklet describes the role of the teacher as follows:

"A Teacher isn't a Bible expert, but — has professional help and guidance. Curriculum materials do not assume that teachers are Bible authorities. Resource materials provide thorough Bible background. Staff members are always ready to help.

"A Teacher doesn't know all the answers, but — is a learner among learners. The teaching process emphasizes the teacher as a guide — a fellow discoverer. The teacher is not embarrassed if he does not know the answer. He says, "Let's find out together."

"A Teacher isn't tied to a rigid programme, but — is free to be creative and flexible.

The teacher can make use of his own special talents and avoid those areas which he finds difficult or awkward. The teacher may call upon other people with special skills or resources for some parts of the programme.

*This material is quoted from a booklet prepared by Mrs. Donna Mason, Director of Christian Education at Fremont Presbyterian Church in Sacramento, California.

"A Teacher doesn't teach a curriculum, but — teaches people.
The teacher attempts to meet the needs of each student. Students remember teachers long after the lessons themselves have been forgotten. God works through people to reveal his love and truth.

"A Teacher doesn't teach all the time, but — takes time to listen.
Maybe this is the only place a child can talk to an adult who listens and really cares.''

"A Teacher doesn't do it alone, but — is part of a team.
Life together in the church is team-work. Teaching in the church requires team-work between teachers and students, between teachers and other teachers, and between teachers and other staff.''

6. *Instead of expecting teachers to learn how to teach by teaching, provide a regular programme of pre-service and in-service training.*
There are many ways to provide training for teachers which are developed further in this chapter. However, consider the following:

a. Provide an annual ''Introduction to Church Teaching'' course to introduce the roles and skills of teaching. This course could be part of a regular adult education programme and offered to parents, new members, older youth and others who are potential teachers.
b. Encourage people to get acquainted with teaching by serving as teacher's aides for a short period of time.
c. Maintain an ''open-door policy'' which will encourage other people to feel free to visit church classes to observe teaching in action.
d. Publish a quarterly or annual list of all training opportunities that are available locally, regionally, denominationally or through other agencies.

7. *Instead of recruiting teachers and leaving them on their own or forgetting about them, take steps to make sure that their work is recognized.*
Teachers will hardly ever ask to be recognized. They should not have to ask. Ministers and other church members can find many ways to provide recognition of the teaching staff. It is important to the whole church that the teaching ministry be visible. Programmes will never be established as a high priority for financial support unless they are visible and obviously worthwhile. Some ways to recognize teachers include:

a. Write-ups of teachers and/or class activities in the weekly bulletin and/or monthly newsletter.

b. List teachers with others on the official church notice-boards.

c. An annual "open day".

d. An annual reception for teachers.

e. A service of dedication for the teaching staff.

f. Displays, exhibitions and reports of student activities, projects and creative work.

g. Sharing of student-produced materials with other church groups or in worship services.

h. Inviting representatives of the teaching staff to make brief informal reports to the official church meetings several times a year.

i. Occasional phone calls or personal visits to teachers by someone on the church staff.

What is suggested above is just an outline of some possibilities for increasing the visibility, the importance, and the place of teaching in the church. The main point is that each church must develop a strategy that places teachers and teaching at the centre of the church's concern for effective ministry. The challenge is for you to work with a few other concerned, responsible people to review your present strategy and/or develop a more appropriate strategy.

C. Types of teacher education events

Once a church has developed a strategy for the recruiting, recognition and support of teachers it is important to include in that strategy a systematic programme of teacher education.

There are many types of teacher education events, some of which are outlined below. Also, the first twelve chapters of this book could be used as guidelines for a programme of teacher education.

What follows is a list of a wide variety of types of training events that can be offered to church teachers. These suggestions are not evaluated or placed in any particular order.

1. Brief training period as part of the regular teachers' meeting.

If teachers meet monthly or on some other regular basis it is possible to spend thirty to ninety minutes of that meeting on a specific resource, method, activity, skill, or concept related to the teaching task.

2. Teacher briefing sessions for all teachers of one age group.

When two or more teachers are teaching the same material in one or more

churches, they can meet together once per unit to receive help from each other and to discuss the next unit of study.

3. The "one-night-stand" event.

One event of two or three hours scheduled for a group of teachers. These are the most difficult to conduct. There is little continuity between previous or succeeding events.

4. The series approach.

Several events conducted weekly or monthly for a period of time. Each event is related to the others so that the whole series provides a systematic development of basic topics and skills.

5. Intensive, developmental approach.

Six or more events conducted in a relatively short period of time – two weekends, one week, or two nights each for three weeks. The basic components of the teaching-learning process are identified, practised, and evaluated.

6. Small group, laboratory approach.

A number of sessions with small groups of teachers representing similar age groups of students. Focus is upon the specific needs of the teachers as identified by the leader and the teachers themselves. Work involves practice and observation of classroom teaching.

7. Repeatable experiences.

One or more sessions providing specific experiences that can be repeated in the classroom. Focus may be on content, teaching procedures, or use of equipment and resources.

8. The "friend system"

Many church teachers know at least one school teacher who teaches the same age group. Many professional teachers feel unable to teach on Sunday as well. But many of these same teachers would be more than willing to consult with a church teacher on a regular basis. If a church teacher were to seek out a professional teacher to be his or her "friend" for a year a lot of good things could happen.

○ The church teacher could observe several times in a school classroom.

○ The two teachers could meet together occasionally for consultation and planning.

○ The school teacher could observe in the church class and provide some helpful evaluation and constructive criticism.

When one sees a list such as the one above, it seems obvious that we should never feel limited in what we offer to our teachers. It is also obvious that no one type of training event will ever meet all the needs of even one teacher, let alone a whole teaching staff in one or more churches. Whoever is responsible for providing teacher education events for teachers must develop a stategy that will incorporate many approaches of teacher education and will encourage the teachers to be selective and respond to what they find of interest to them, of value in meeting their needs, and most convenient in terms of the time and location of the event. If church teachers are to become better equipped to teach, then a well-defined, promoted and implemented strategy must be developed that will reach the teachers where they are, in their local communities with specific needs and responsibilities.

D. Teacher education for churches without any trained teachers

Teaching effectiveness in all churches is not going to improve unless more time, energy, money and commitment are invested in equipping teachers with insights, skills, resources, and motivation that will enable them to do a better job.

What follows is an outline of several strategies that could be considered by churches in order to provide teacher education services to their teachers.

1. Several churches of different denominations in one town or several churches of one denomination in a geographical area could combine personnel, money, and resources in order to:

a. establish a teacher education committee to plan, promote and implement a teacher education programme;

b. develop a media resource centre to pool all media resources and purchase new materials that could serve all the churches; and

c. form a "leadership pool" by identifying and enlisting people in the churches and community with special skills who could provide training or assistance to teachers in specific skills or subject areas.

2. A church could identify and enlist two or three people from the church membership who have had experience with teaching and provide them with specialized training in order to serve as leaders of teacher education in their church.

3. A minister who is interested and skilled in church education could enlist several people to work with him to provide teacher education. The minister could provide teacher briefing on the subject matter for a unit of study, and one or two other people could provide the briefing regarding teaching activities and resources for the same unit of study.

4. A teacher education co-ordinator or small committee could work on providing a "friend" for each teacher on the staff. (See Section C, item 8.)

It should be apparent that any of the above could be used by itself but that several of the strategies when used together in a co-ordinated way would provide for maximum effectiveness.

The primary implication is that someone, or several people, in a church must become aware of the need for teacher education in their church and assume responsibility for implementing a helpful programme. There needs to be an overall co-operative, co-ordinated strategy developed by each church. It is often most helpful for several churches to work together.

E. Necessary components of all teacher education events

In conducting teacher education events for groups of between thirty and three hundred people representing a wide spectrum of denominational affiliations, I have concluded for myself that the following methods work best.

1. Take the stance that "we are all in this together." No one is an expert. We are all teachers with more or less experience than the other, but each one of us wants to become more skilful in teaching. Keep the workshop low-key, so that people are helped to feel comfortable about themselves, each other, and their tasks as teachers.

2. Keep lecture presentations to a minimum. In a three-hour workshop, thirty to forty minutes of lecture would be the maximum.

3. Involve people in experiencing teaching activities and resources. Refer to these direct experiences as examples of important educational principles.

4. Plan for teaching activities that people can adapt and use in their own teaching situations.

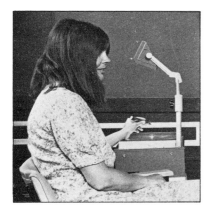

5. Provide many opportunities for people to interact with each other in small groups. Plan for small groups to report or share with the whole group the results of their discussion, research, or creativity.

6. Use a variety of media resources during the workshop.

7. Duplicate materials that can be distributed to people to take home with them.

8. Provide several tables of display materials and resources for people to browse and preview.

9. Use a large room for the workshop. Arrange the room with people seated comfortably at tables.

10. Use an overhead projector as a means to provide visual communication by using prepared transparencies, displaying small group reports, recording responses by participants, or illustrating key concepts.

11. Plan the training event so that the method used for the event will in itself be a teaching point, as well as the actual content of the event.

12. Respond to people when they have said or done something in a way that will give them positive encouragement.

13. Encourage people to express themselves freely and creatively by being open to what they have to say.

14. The workshop should be practical in every way, so that the experienced teacher can build on what is offered and the inexperienced teacher can be helped to implement the things they learn.

Just as teaching is an art, so is designing and leading teacher education events. Many people have attended a lot of training events from which they have received very little practical help. After attending a teacher education event, all the participants have the right to expect that they will be able to do something different the next week in their classroom. Those who lead teacher education events need to set high standards for themselves so that they will prepare carefully and provide helpful leadership for every event.

F. Ten descriptions of teacher education events

The following descriptions represent what I believe to be some of the more important subjects for teacher education events. Subject matter and resources for most of these ten events are included in the first twelve chapters of this book. Each of these events could be conducted in a minimum of three hours. However, it is possible to take parts of each event for a shorter period of time or to expand each event for three or more extra hours. It is assumed that each event would be led by one person. However, it would be possible for a team of two or three leaders to conduct each event. What is presented in each description is what I include in the training events I conduct under these titles.

You will want to add, subtract, and adapt the descriptions to fit your situation and to represent your concerns. There are many ways to design each event to achieve the objectives as they are stated.

1. Planning for teaching
A 3 hour workshop for teachers

Many teachers' manuals contain more than it is possible to teach, and many teachers need help in deciding what to teach in a given situation.

Learning experiences for students of all ages need to be planned creatively in order to motivate and involve students as they study and make discoveries for themselves. This workshop will focus upon some very specific steps that teachers can take to plan for creative teaching.

Through this workshop, teachers will be enabled to:

1. Identify key concepts for teaching and be selective of what to teach in a limited time.
2. Determine specific instructional objectives that will guide their planning and the students' activities.
3. Select teaching activities and resources to communicate the key concepts and achieve the objectives.
4. Use several helpful criteria to evaluate their teaching plans.
5. Use specific lesson-planning processes in relation to their own curriculum.

2. Team teaching in church education
A 3 hour workshop

One feature of the Christian community is that people share together the responsibility for the whole ministry and mission of the church. In church education there are many very positive values to team teaching that provide support for the teachers as well as enhance students' learning. It is important to equip teachers to serve effectively in teaching teams.

In this workshop participants will:

1. Develop a workable definition of team teaching that can be implemented in their own situations.
2. Experience several examples of team planning and decision-making.
3. Review several alternative models of team planning and teaching.
4. Discuss their own needs and desires regarding their role as teachers.
5. Consider a checklist of ten steps for effective team planning and teaching.

Resources used in this workshop could include a filmstrip, and one or two simulation games (such as *Teacher Survival,* page 36).

3. God through the eyes of a child
A 3 hour workshop

Teachers and parents are more effective when they are able to understand God, the Church, the Bible, and the world from the frame of reference of those whom they teach. Children start with primitive concepts and grow in their understanding of God. They are not able to understand adult concepts. Therefore, adults must work extra hard to look at abstract concepts through the eyes of children.

Participants in this workshop will:

1. Hear a brief presentation on the conceptual development of children.
2. Explore ways children grow in their thinking about God.
3. Identify some of the difficult questions that children ask their parents and teachers.
4. Preview a variety of resources that can be used in teaching children in church and at home.
5. Consider some ways children have expressed their ideas about God, Jesus, the Church, and the Bible through creative writing and art.

4. Increasing teacher-student interaction
A 5-6 hour workshop

Much teaching in the church relies upon the spoken words of both the teachers and the students. Most observers of church teaching report that teachers do 75-90 per cent of the talking that occurs in the classroom. It is true that students are most motivated to learn when they themselves are actively involved. There are many ways teachers can increase student involvement.

This workshop will enable participants to:

1. Identify ten categories of teacher-student talk and to use the process of Verbal Interaction Analysis as a tool for evaluation of classroom talk.
2. Employ several basic rules in developing verbal and written instructions for classroom activities.
3. Identify three general categories of questions and prepare questions in each category.
4. Develop a checklist of a dozen principles to follow when engaging students in interaction.
5. Work with other teachers to improve their skills of giving directions, encouraging students, and asking questions.

Several taped, filmed, and programmed resources and activities will be used to involve participants directly in working on the skills necessary to achieve the above objectives.

5. Creative ways
to study and teach the Bible
A 3-10 hour workshop

The Bible is the basic textbook of Christian education in teaching children, youth, and adults. All people should be helped to read, study, and interpret the Bible so that its message becomes relevant to their own lives. It is not enough just to read a few verses and discuss them, or to memorize a few selected verses, or to fill in the blanks in a workbook. Creative studying and teaching of the Bible requires that people develop a few basic skills and have available some basic resources. The most effective way to learn is to be involved directly in the process of exploring scripture and applying its message to contemporary situations.

As a result of participating in this workshop, people will be enabled to:

1. Use several basic skills and resources for their own study of the Bible. (Resources to include: Concordance, footnotes, Dictionary, Commentary and Atlas.)
2. Compare inductive and deductive teaching styles.
3. Identify several basic principles that apply to the teaching of scripture with any age group.
4. Repeat several of the six to ten different experiences of Bible study in their own classroom.
5. State the value of using a variety of media resources in teaching scripture.
6. Decide which resources will be needed for teaching the Bible in their own classroom.

The approaches to teaching the Bible experienced in this workshop are of the same style and approaches as the ones included in *Using the Bible in Teaching* and *Using the Bible with Audio-Visuals.*

6. Translating the Bible
through teaching activities
A 6-9 hour workshop

One of the primary activities of the Christian Church has been the translation of the Holy Scriptures into the languages of the people of every land. Today one of the important areas for translating scripture is in the classroom. Students of all ages need to hear, read, and experience the Scriptures in a ''language'' they can understand and respond to. In many ways the Christian teacher serves as a translator. In order to become effective translators, teachers need to develop skills, use resources, and devise strategies that communicate the Good News. This workshop will involve participants in a wide variety of teaching activities that can be repeated or adapted for use in their own classrooms.

In this workshop participants will:

1. Consider the role of translator as a primary role for Christian teachers.

2. Review ten important decisions every teacher must make in the process of planning and teaching each lesson.

3. Be involved in a series of creative teaching activities focusing on the Old and the New Testaments.

4. Experience two brief simulated activities as models for teaching the Bible.

5. Explore a variety of resources that are available for creative teaching.

This workshop is designed especially for teachers of young adults and adult classes. Teachers of younger children will find helpful insights for their own personal Bible study and will be able to apply many of the basic principles to their own teaching.

7. Creative uses of media
A 3-6 hour workshop for teachers

People today live in a world of media. Homes, schools, churches and other institutions experience the influence of a wide variety of media. People can communicate more effectively and learn more when they are enabled to use all of their senses in the process. Teachers have access to a lot of media already and can with little effort procure or devise many other media resources. This workshop will focus on ways teachers can use media to prepare their own lessons as well as ways to involve students in the use of the same media.

In this workshop, teachers will be enabled to:

1. Use several media resources and equipment.

2. Express in a creative form several key concepts that are related to a future lesson plan.

3. Identify the criteria for selecting and using media.

4. Select several items to recommend for future purchase and use by their church.

5. Recall a dozen or more ways of using several media.

Two or more of the following resources may be selected as the focus for the workshop. Slides without a camera, slides with a camera, cassette tape recordings, overhead projection, filmstrips, 16mm films, teaching pictures and study prints, or records.

8. Ways to involve students in learning
A 6 hour workshop

People learn most effectively when they are actively involved in what they are learning. There are several keys to student involvement in learning activities: motivation, relevance to life experience, variety of teaching activities, and the teacher's role in the classroom. Teachers make many crucial decisions in the process of their planning and while engaged in teaching that influence student involvement. Teachers can be helped to identify these moments of decision and to increase their skilfulness in making helpful decisions.

In this workshop, participants will:

1. Identify several crucial classroom decisions that influence the level of student involvement.
2. Employ several basic rules in developing verbal and written instructions for classroom activities.
3. Compare inductive and deductive teaching style.
4. Identify three general categories of questions and prepare questions in each category.
5. Develop a checklist of a dozen techniques to use when engaging students in their own learning.
6. Experience a variety of ways to approach the teaching of scripture.
7. Work with other teachers in a process of mutual support and constructive criticism to improve their skills of direction-giving, question-asking, decision-making and reinforcement.

9. Teaching values in Christian education
A 3-6 hour workshop

Christian education has always been concerned about helping students to form Christian values. Traditionally the approach to value formation has been moralizing. There is another, more effective approach, developed by Sidney Simon, known as values clarification. This approach involves people directly in the process of clarifying and forming their own values. There are dozens of specific strategies that teachers can use with students which increase their motivation, involvement and learning.

In this workshop, participants will:

1. Compare the differences between the moralizing and clarifying approaches to values formation.
2. Identify the seven steps which result in the formation of a person's values.
3. Experience six to ten different values clarifying strategies that can be used with students.
4. Work on designing their own strategies for values clarification to present to the whole group.
5. Discuss ways to implement values clarification strategies in their regular teaching situations.

The approach of the workshop will attempt to relate values clarification to biblical and theological concepts. This workshop is appropriate to teachers of all age groups and most especially youth.

10. Individualizing instruction through learning centres
A 3-10 hour workshop

Contract learning, individualized instruction and learning centres are approaches to teaching that are gaining wider acceptance in education. The focus of these approaches is to design learning activities appropriate to the skills, interests, and needs of the students and to motivate students to participate directly in deciding what they will do to increase their learning. The role of the teacher becomes primarily that of planner, manager and facilitator of learning activities. Also, the teacher is more free to respond to individual students. These approaches to teaching that lead to a more open classroom can increase the effectiveness of Christian teaching.

As a result of participating in this workshop, people will:

1. Experience directly one or more learning centres or self-instructional modules.
2. Discuss the implications of individualizing instruction for Christian teaching.
3. Design one learning centre activity or self-instructional module.
4. Preview a variety of resources available to guide teachers in planning for individualizing instruction.

Bibliography

Resources from the Bible Society

The Bible Society has many resources to help you to use the Bible in teaching. We can supply you with:
Bibles, New Testaments, Portions, scriptures on cassette, film strips, slides, records and many other things.

Write for a catalogue containing details of all our materials to:
The Development Consultant
Bible Society
146 Queen Victoria Street
LONDON EC4V 4BX

Here are some useful books for use by leaders and students involved in Christian Education.

Bible concordances and encyclopaedias

Cruden's Complete Concordance: Lutterworth Press
The Bible Reader's Encyclopaedia and Concordance: Collins
Young's Analytical Concordance: Lutterworth Press
RSV Handy Concordance: Pickering and Inglis
The Lion Encyclopedia of the Bible: Lion Publishing
Analytical Concordance to the RSV of the New Testament by Morrison: Westminster
Nelson's Complete Concordance to the RSV: Nelson
Modern Concordance to the New Testament: Darton, Longman & Todd.

Bible dictionaries

Concise Dictionary of the Bible: Lutterworth Press
Black's Bible Dictionary: A & C Black
The New Bible Dictionary: IVP
Vine's Expository Dictionary: Oliphants
Dictionary of Bible People/Words/Times: Scripture Union
Revell's Dictionary of Bible People: Revell.

Bible commentaries

The New Bible Commentary (Revised) by Guthrie, Motyer, Stibbs and Wiseman: IVP
A Bible Commentary for Today by Howley, Bruce and Ellison: Pickering and Inglis
Tyndale Commentaries (single volumes on individual books): IVP
Black's New Testament Commentaries (individual books): A & C Black, London
Cambridge Bible Commentary (individual books): Cambridge University Press
The New Century Bible (individual books)
SCM Pelican Commentaries (individual books): Pelican Books

The Good News according to Mark by E. Schweizer: SPCK
Peake's Commentary (one volume): Nelson

For background reading

The Living World of the Old Testament by B. W. Anderson: Longman
Introducing the New Testament by A. M. Hunter: SCM Press
A New 'Testament History by Floyd Filson: SCM Press
Mark — Evangelist and Theologian by R. P. Martin: Paternoster
Luke — Historian and Theologian by H. Marshall: Paternoster
The Lion Handbook to the Bible: Lion Publishing
The History of Christianity: Lion Publishing
Lion Photo-Guides to the Old and New Testaments: Lion Publishing
Paul by John Drane: Lion Publishing
Jesus by John Drane: Lion Publishing
Concise Bible Atlas: Paternoster Press
New Testament Introduction by Guthrie: IVP
Understanding the New Testament Series (separate volumes on individual books): Scripture Union
The Good News in . . . Series (separate volumes on individual books): Fontana
Values Clarification: A Handbook of Practical Strategies for Teachers and Students by Sidney B. Simon, et. al.: Hart Publishing Co., Inc., New York (1972).
Preparing Instructional Objectives by Robert F. Mager: Fearson Publishers, Palo Alto (1972).
Designing Instructional Text by James Hartley: Kogan Page
Taxonomy of Educational Objectives Handbooks 1 & 2: by Benjamin S. Bloom: Longman.

Audio-visual resources

Filmstrips, cassettes, slide productions and records are available from:

Church Army Audio-Visual Resources
Church Army Headquarters
Independents Road
Blackheath
London SE3 9LG

National Christian Education Council
Robert Denholm House
Nutfield
Redhill
Surrey RH1 4HW

Falcon Audio Visual Aids
Falcon Court
32 Fleet Street
London EC4Y 1DB

Concordia Films
Viking Way
Bar Hill Village
Cambridge CB3 8EL

Sound and Vision Unit
Scripture Union House
130 City Road
London EC1V 2NJ

Lion Publishing
Icknield Way
Tring
Herts HP23 4LE

Write to them for details.

"Write-on Film" and "Ektagraphic" pre-mounted slides are produced by Kodak Ltd, and are available from Opsis, 134 London Road, Southborough, Tonbridge, Kent.